FOR ORGANS, PIANOS & ELECTRONIC KEYBOARDS

E-Z PLAY TODAY

155

THE BEST OF BILLY JOEL

T0033986

CONTENTS

ISBN 978-0-7935-1118-1

HAL•LEONARD
CORPORATION

7777 W. BLUEMOUND RD. P.O. BOX 13819 MILWAUKEE, WI 53213

E-Z Play ® TODAY Music Notation © 1975 HAL LEONARD PUBLISHING CORPORATION
Copyright © 1992 by HAL LEONARD PUBLISHING CORPORATION
International Copyright Secured   All Rights Reserved

For all works contained herein:
Unauthorized copying, arranging, adapting, recording or public performance is an infringement of copyright.
Infringers are liable under the law.

E-Z PLAY and EASY ELECTRONIC KEYBOARD MUSIC are registered trademarks of HAL LEONARD PUBLISHING CORPORATION.

And So It Goes

Registration 10
Rhythm: Waltz

Words and Music by
Billy Joel

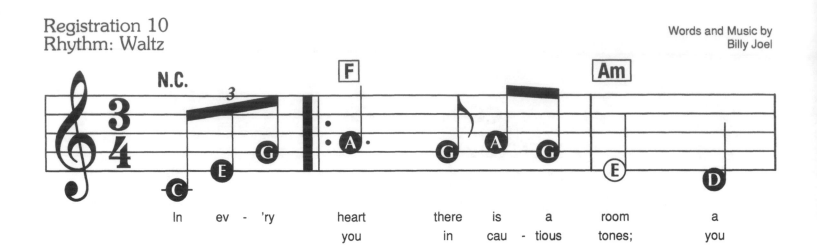

In ev - 'ry heart there is a room a
you in cau - tious tones; you

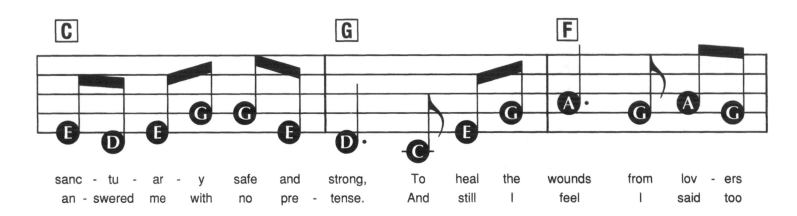

sanc - tu - ar - y safe and strong, To heal the wounds from lov - ers
an - swered me with no pre - tense. And still I feel I said too

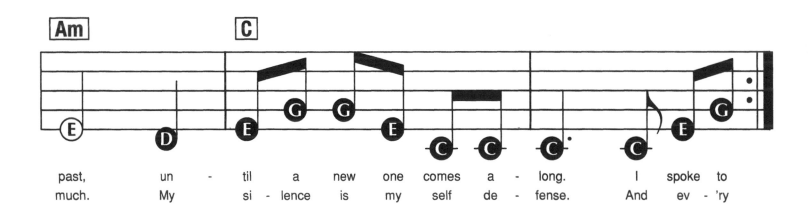

past, un - til a new one comes a - long. I spoke to
much. My si - lence is my self de - fense. And ev - 'ry

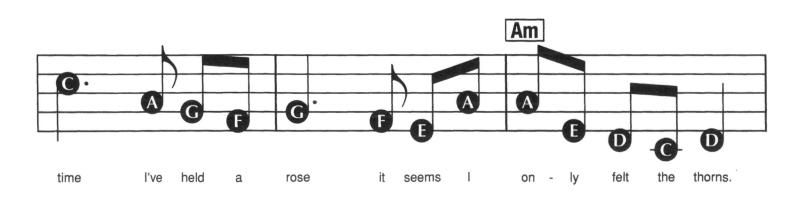

time I've held a rose it seems I on - ly felt the thorns.

© 1983 JOEL SONGS
All Rights Controlled and Administered by EMI BLACKWOOD MUSIC INC.
All Rights Reserved International Copyright Secured Used by Permission

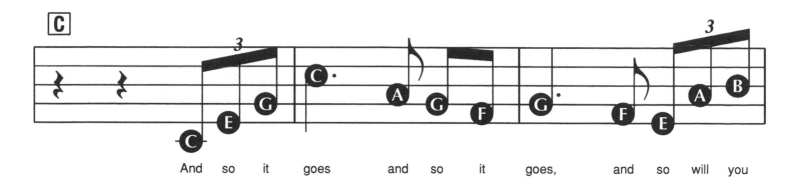

And so it goes and so it goes, and so will you

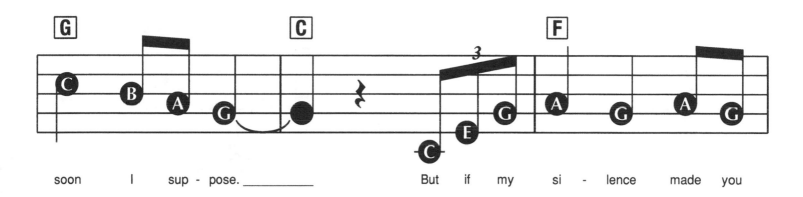

soon I sup - pose. _____ But if my si - lence made you

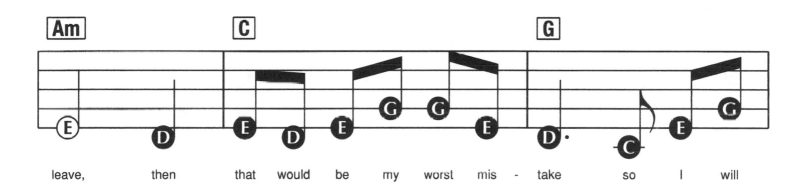

leave, then that would be my worst mis - take so I will

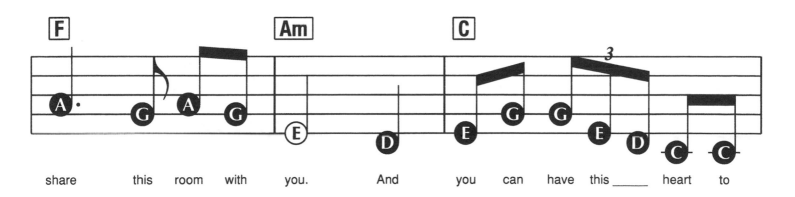

share this room with you. And you can have this ____ heart to

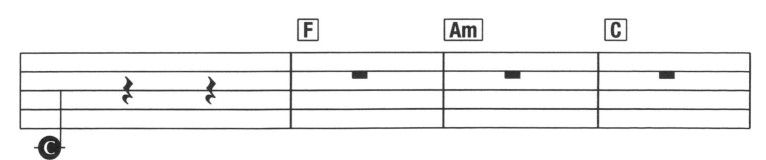

break.

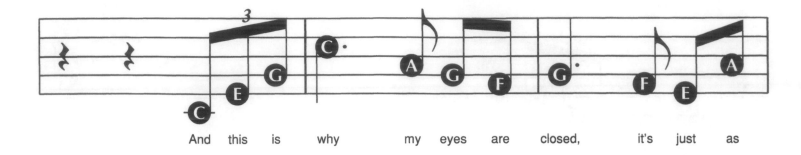

And this is why my eyes are closed, it's just as

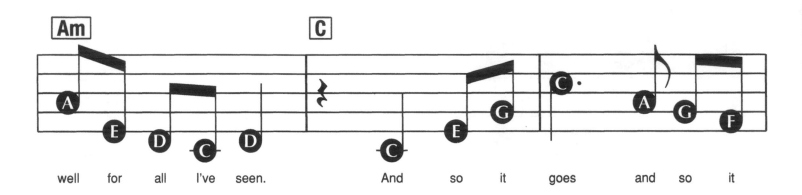

well for all I've seen. And so it goes and so it

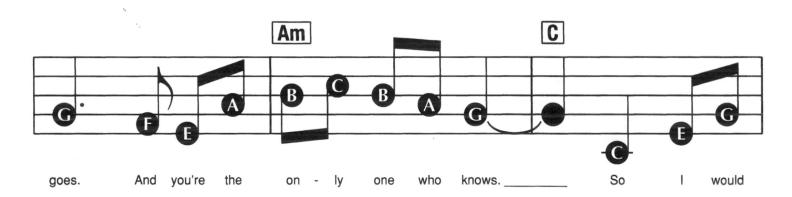

goes. And you're the on - ly one who knows. _____ So I would

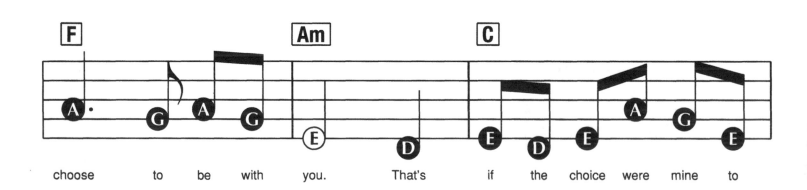

choose to be with you. That's if the choice were mine to

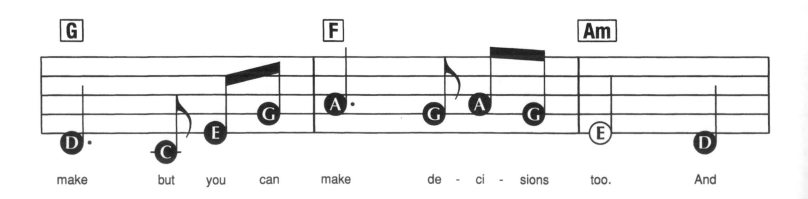

make but you can make de - ci - sions too. And

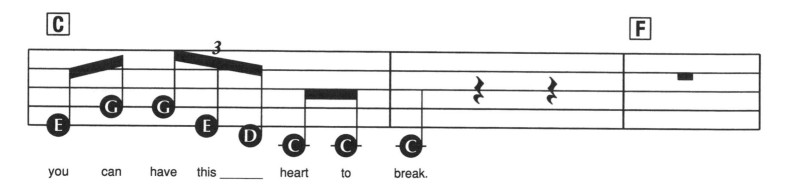

you   can   have   this _____   heart   to   break.

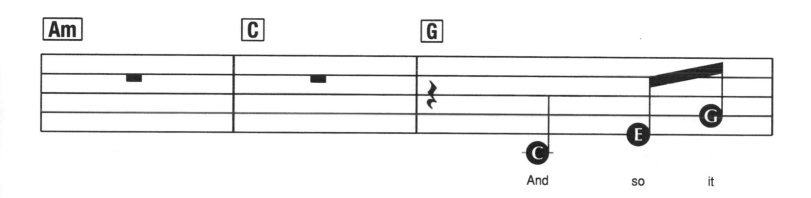

And   so   it

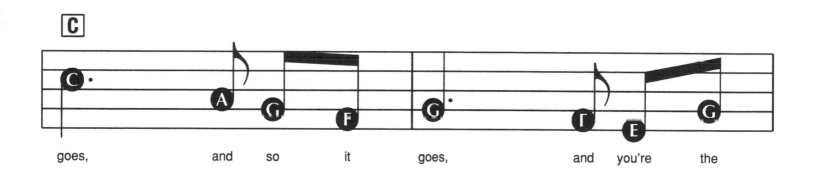

goes,   and   so   it   goes,   and   you're   the

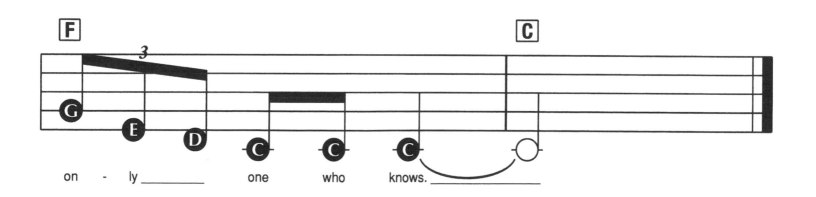

on - ly _____   one   who   knows. _____

Baby Grand

Registration 5
Rhythm: Ballad or Swing

Words and Music by
Billy Joel

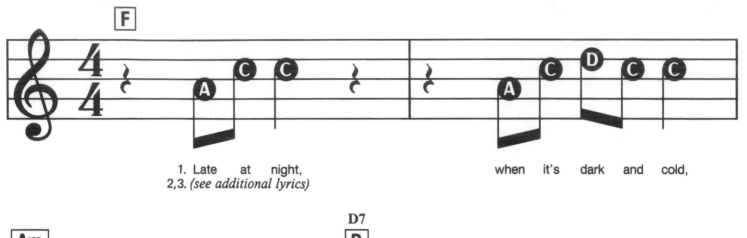

1. Late at night,
2,3. (see additional lyrics)
when it's dark and cold,

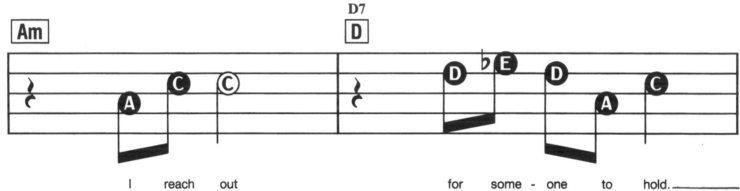

I reach out for some - one to hold.____

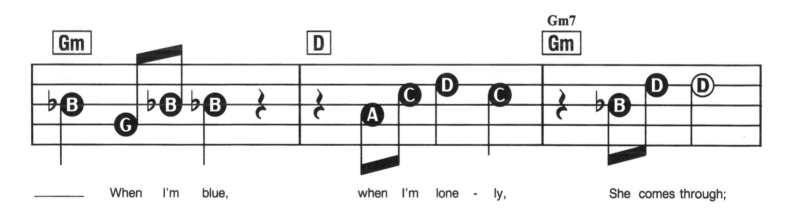

____ When I'm blue, when I'm lone - ly, She comes through;

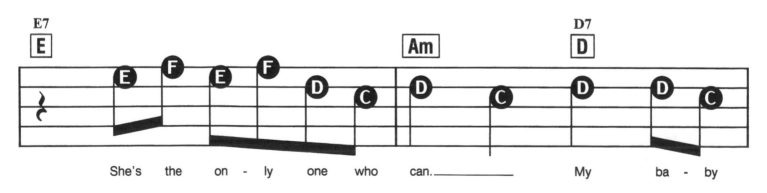

She's the on - ly one who can.____ My ba - by

© 1986 JOEL SONGS
All Rights Controlled and Administered by EMI BLACKWOOD MUSIC INC.
All Rights Reserved   International Copyright Secured   Used by Permission

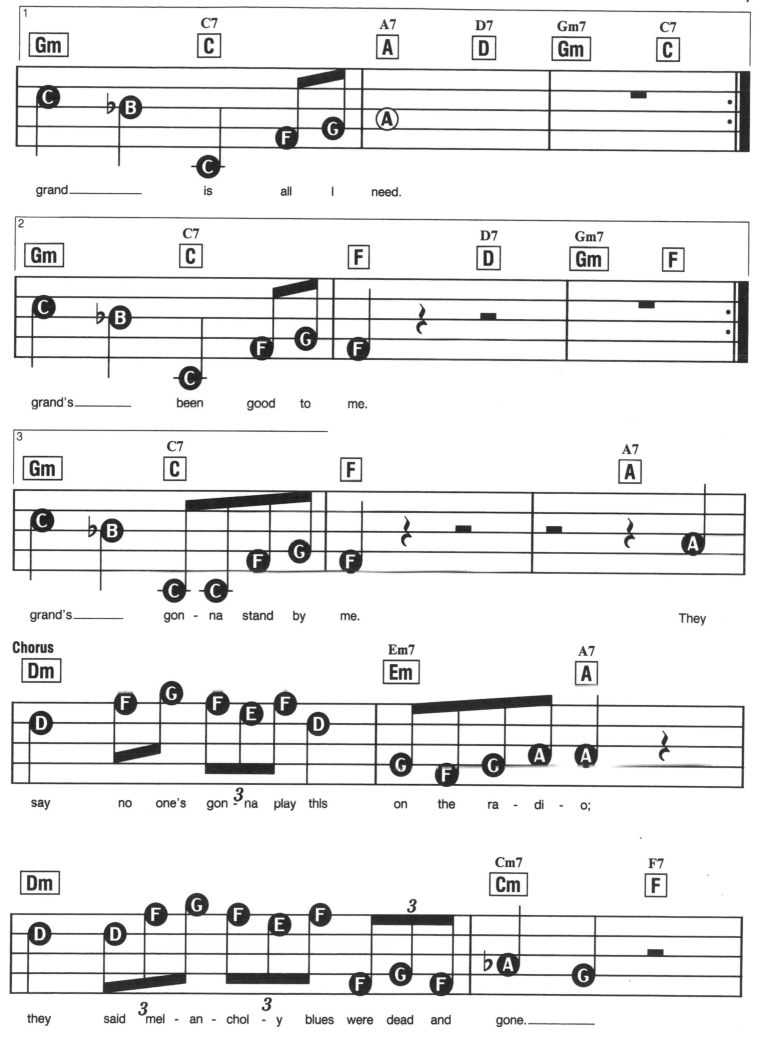

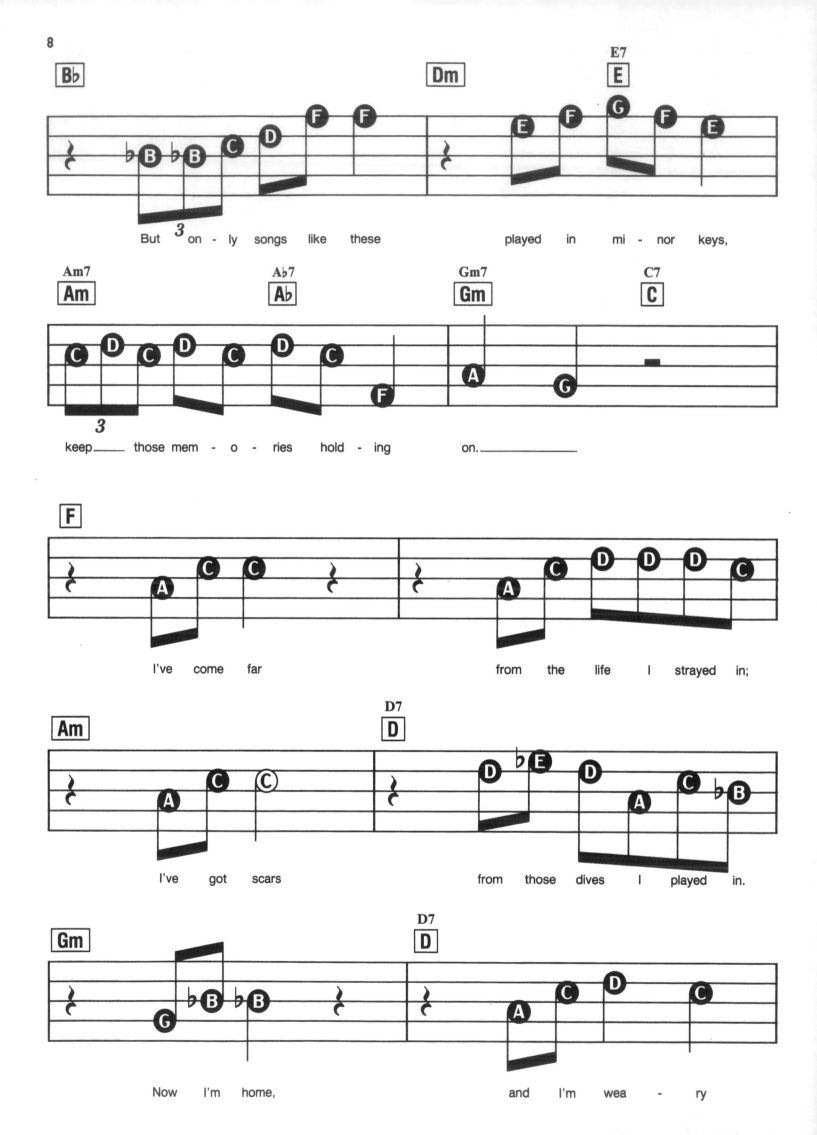

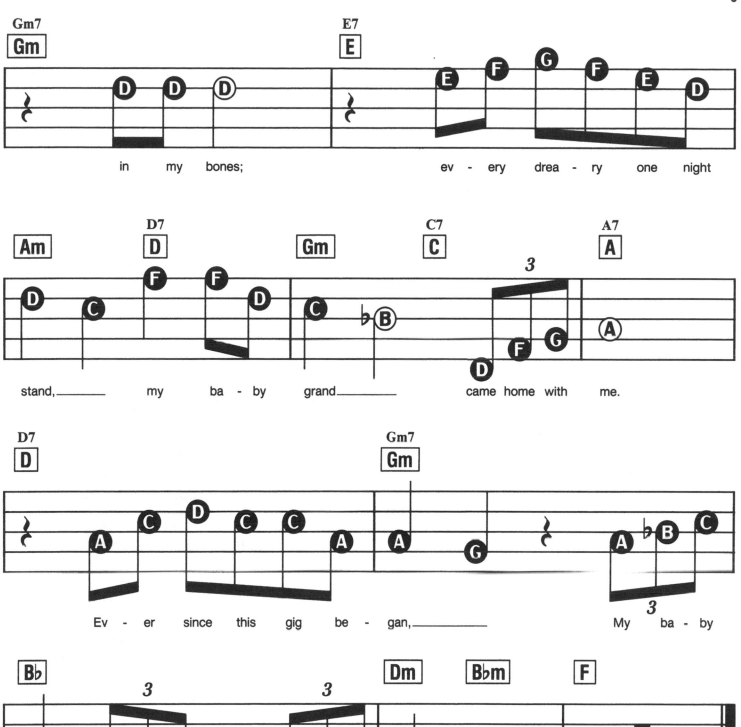

Additional Lyrics

2. In my time, I've wandered everywhere
Around this world; she would always be there,
Any day, any hour;
All it takes is the power in my hands.
This baby grand's been good to me.

3. I've had friends, but they slipped away.
I've had fame, but it doesn't stay.
I've made fortunes, spent them fast enough.
As for women, they don't last with just one man;
But Baby Grand will stand by me.

CHORUS

Honesty

Registration 4
Rhythm: Rock

Words and Music by
Billy Joel

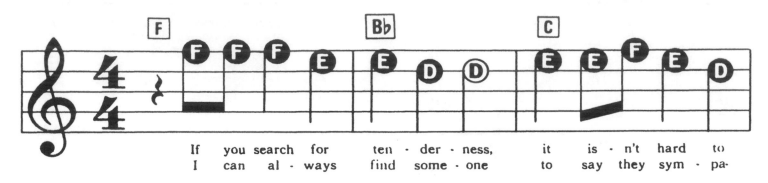

If you search for ten · der · ness, it is · n't hard to
I can al · ways find some · one to say they sym · pa-

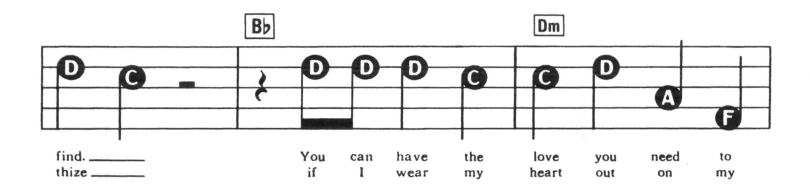

find. _____ You can have the love you need to
thize _____ if I have wear my love heart out on my

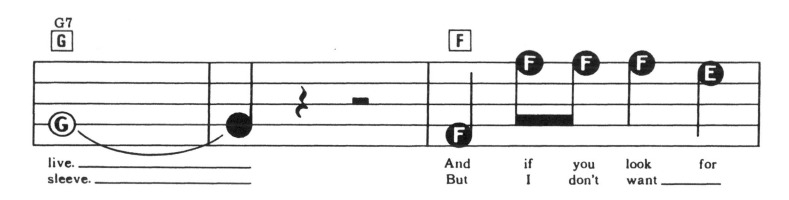

live. _____ And if you look for
sleeve. _____ But I don't want _____

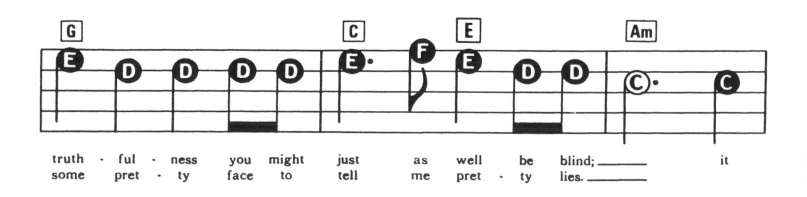

truth · ful · ness you might just as well be blind; _____ it
some pret · ty face to tell me pret · ty lies. _____

© 1978 IMPULSIVE MUSIC
All Rights Controlled and Administered by EMI APRIL MUSIC INC.
All Rights Reserved International Copyright Secured Used by Permission

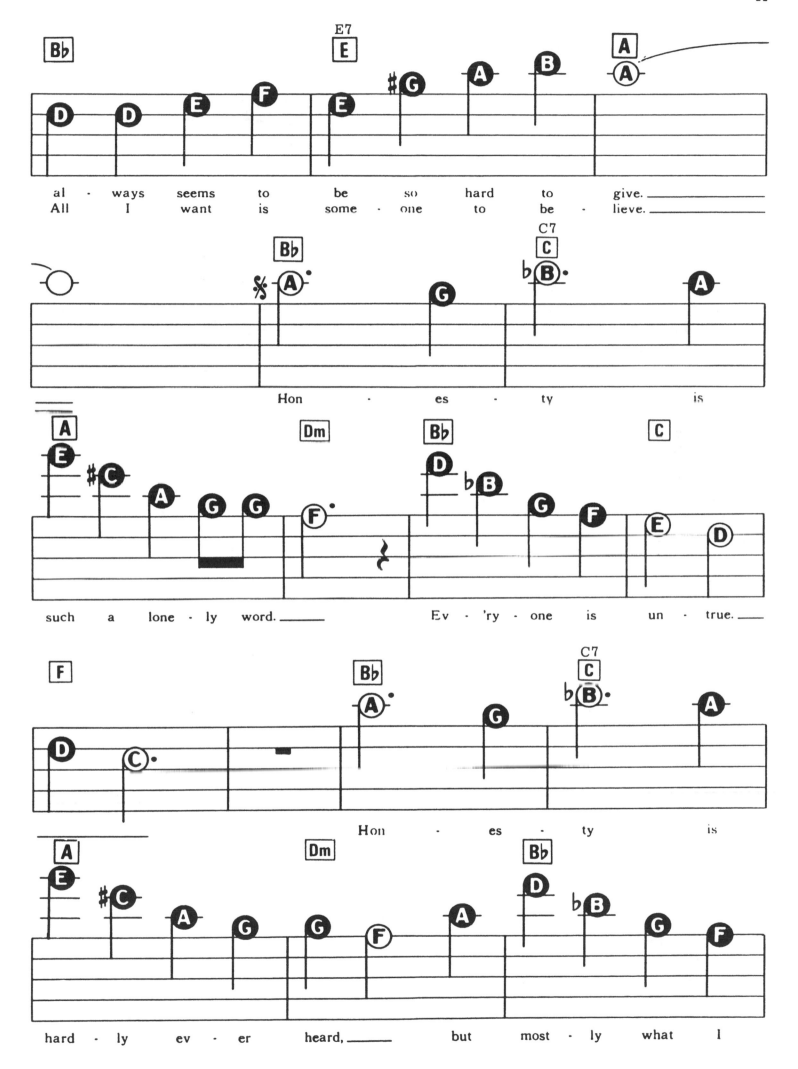

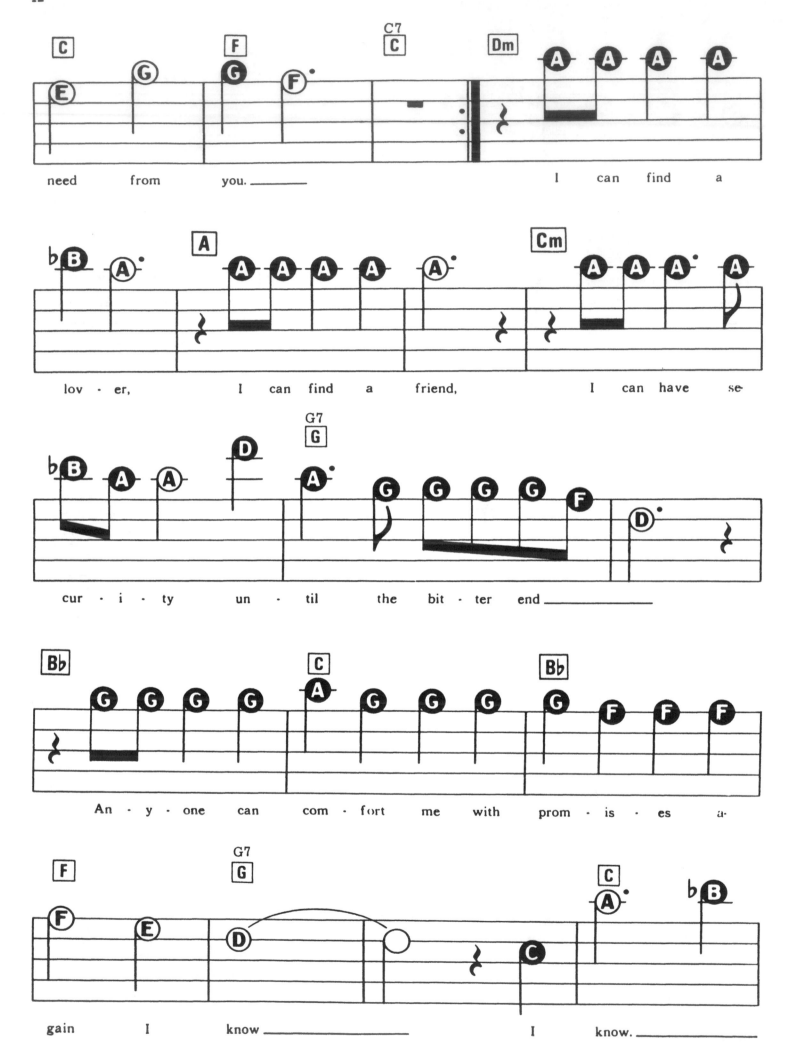

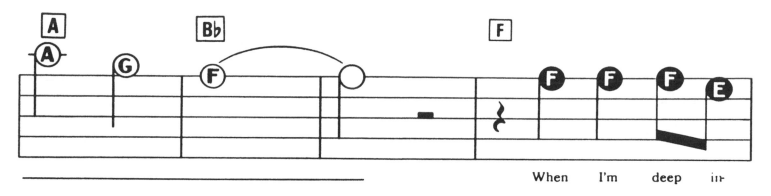

When I'm deep in

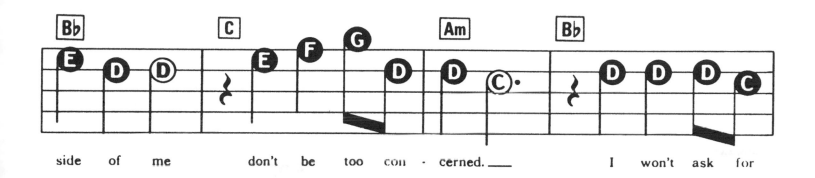

side of me don't be too con - cerned. ___ I won't ask for

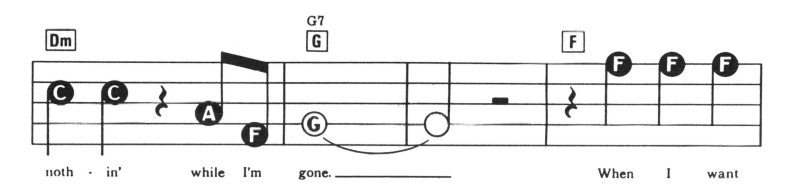

noth - in' while I'm gone. _____ When I want

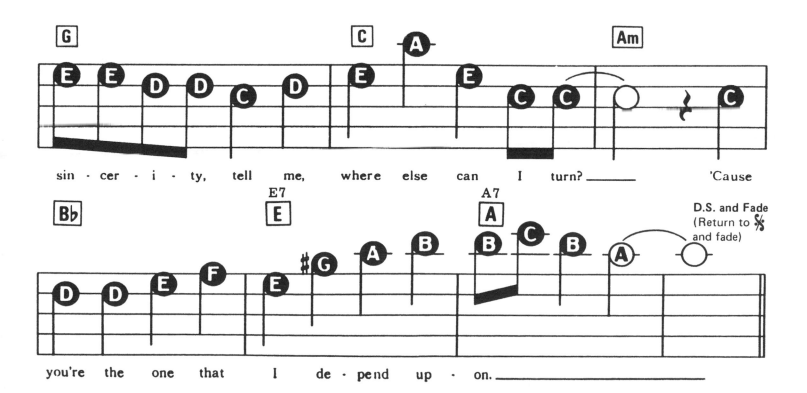

sin - cer - i - ty, tell me, where else can I turn? _____ 'Cause

you're the one that I de - pend up - on. _____

An Innocent Man

Registration 2
Rhythm: Latin or Samba

Words and Music by
Billy Joel

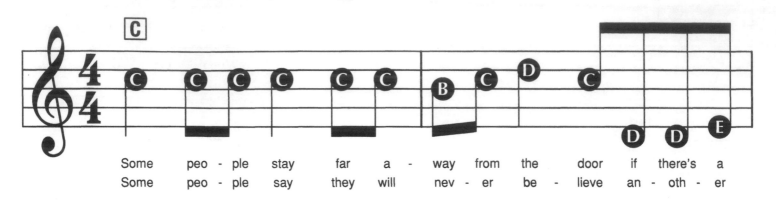

Some peo - ple stay far a - way from the door if there's a
Some peo - ple say they will nev - er be - lieve an - oth - er

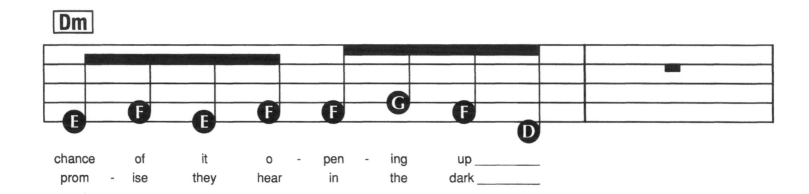

chance of it o - pen - ing up _____
prom - ise they hear in the dark _____

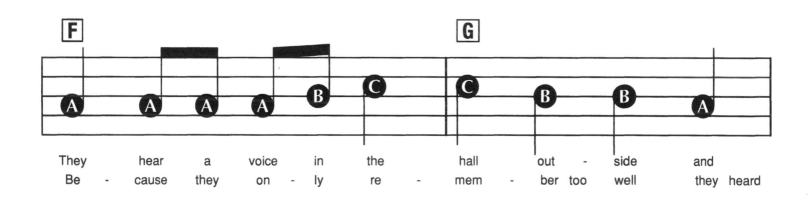

They hear a voice in the hall out - side and
Be - cause they on - ly re - mem - ber too well they heard

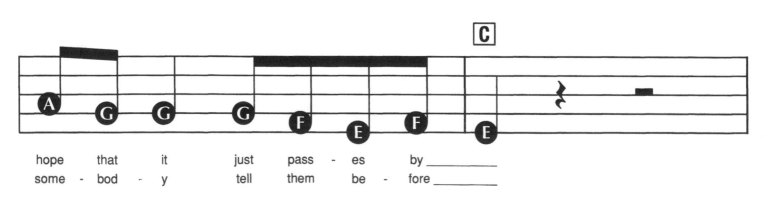

hope that it just pass - es by _____
some - bod - y tell them be - fore _____

© 1983 JOEL SONGS
All Rights Controlled and Administered by EMI BLACKWOOD MUSIC INC.
All Rights Reserved   International Copyright Secured   Used by Permission

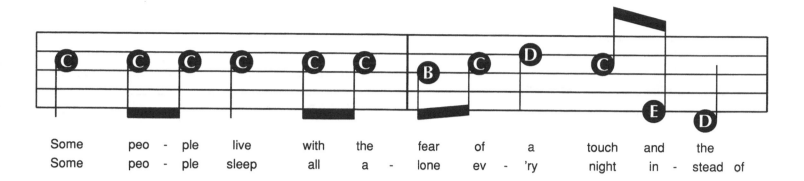

Some peo - ple live with the fear of a touch and the
Some peo - ple sleep all a - lone ev - 'ry night in - stead of

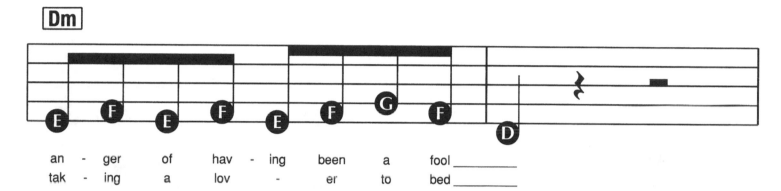

an - ger of hav - ing been a fool _____
tak - ing a lov - er to bed _____

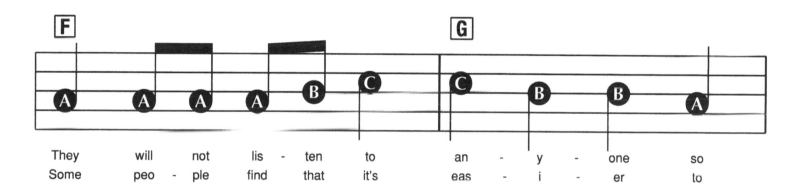

They will not lis - ten to an - y - one so
Some peo - ple find that it's eas - i - er to

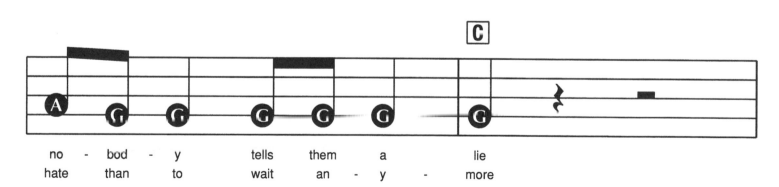

no - bod - y tells them a lie
hate than to wait an - y - more

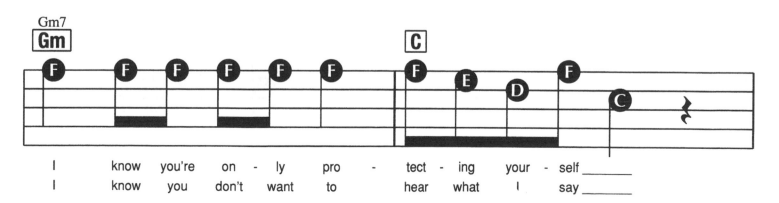

I know you're on - ly pro - tect - ing your - self _____
I know you don't want to hear what I say _____

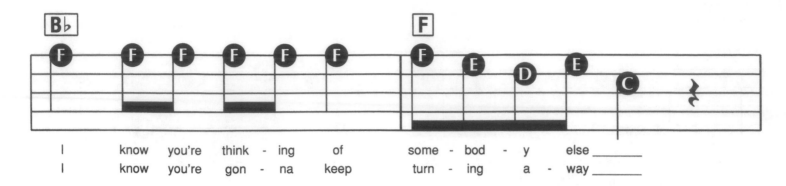

I know you're think - ing of some - bod - y else _____
I know you're gon - na keep turn - ing a - way _____

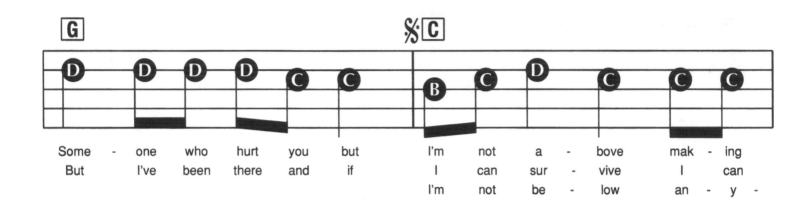

Some - one who hurt you but I'm not a - bove mak - ing
But I've who been there and if I can sur - vive I can
I'm not be - low an - y -

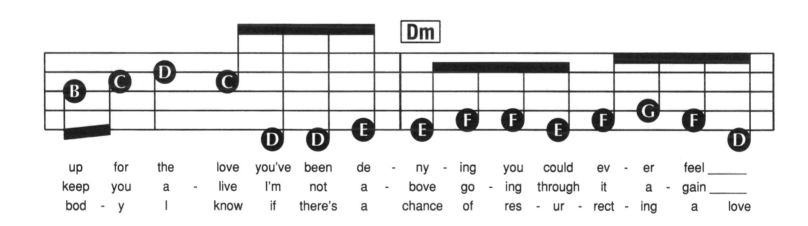

up for the love you've been de - ny - ing you could ev - er feel _____
keep you a - live I'm not a - bove go - ing through it a - gain _____
bod - y I know if there's a chance of res - ur - rect - ing a love

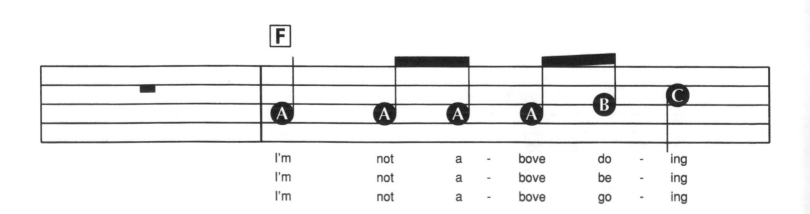

I'm not a - bove do - ing
I'm not a - bove be - ing
I'm not a - bove go - ing

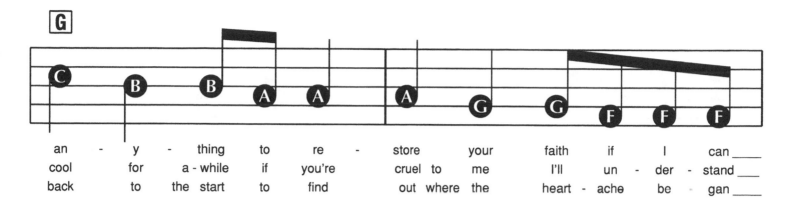

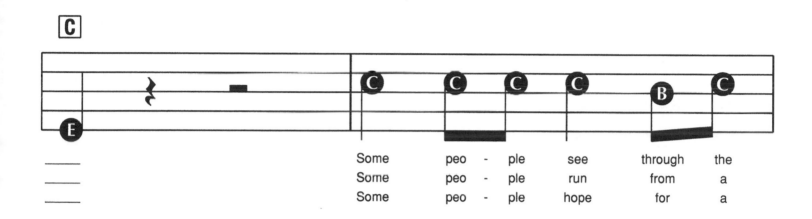

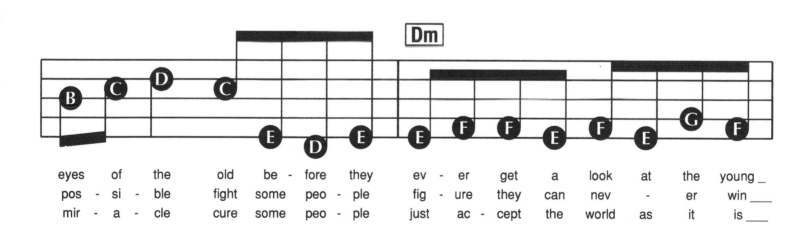

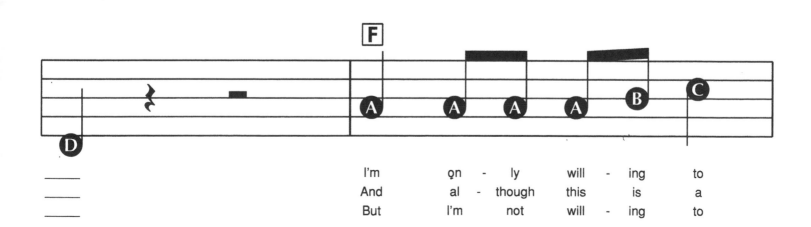

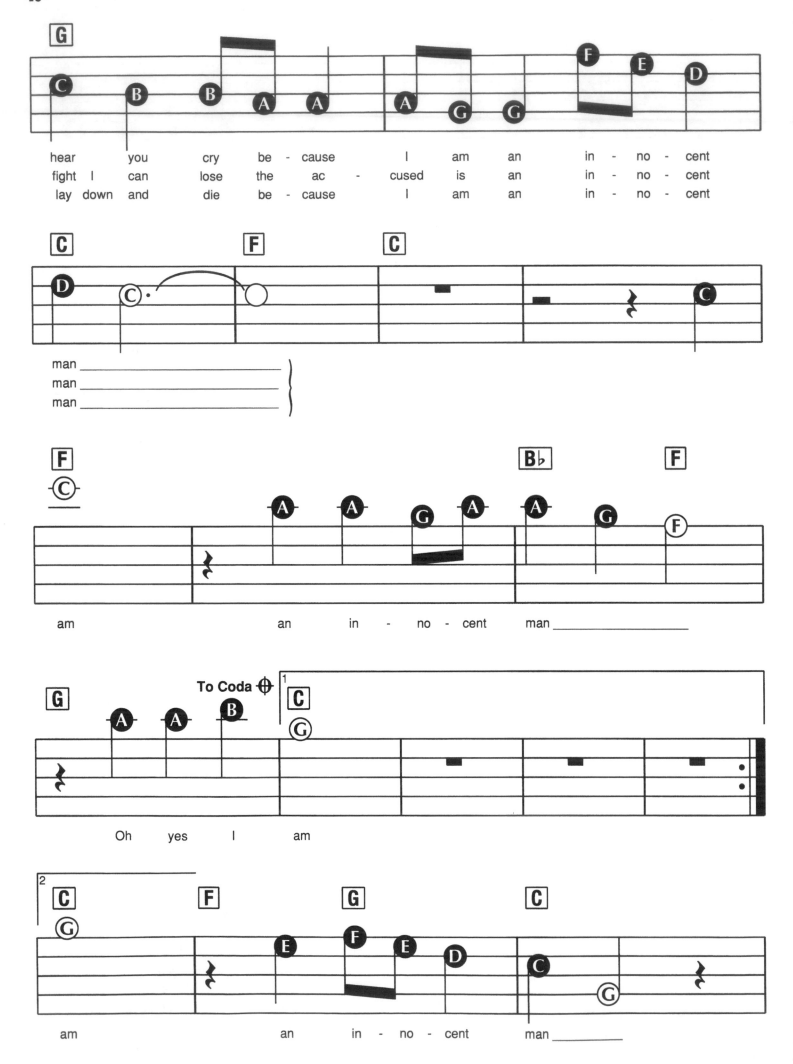

hear   you   cry   be - cause   I   am   an   in - no - cent
fight I can lose   the   ac -   cused   is   an   in - no - cent
lay down and die   be - cause   I   am   an   in - no - cent

man _____
man _____
man _____

am   an   in - no - cent   man _____

Oh   yes   I   am

am   an   in - no - cent   man _____

19

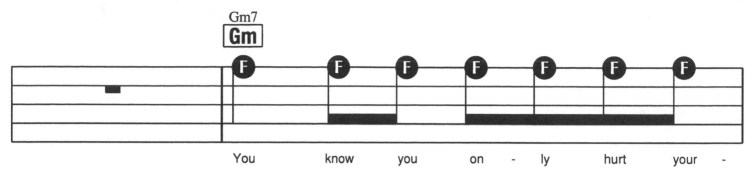

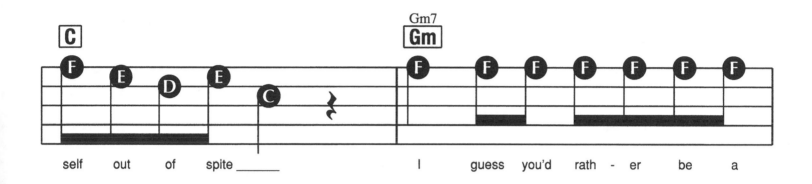

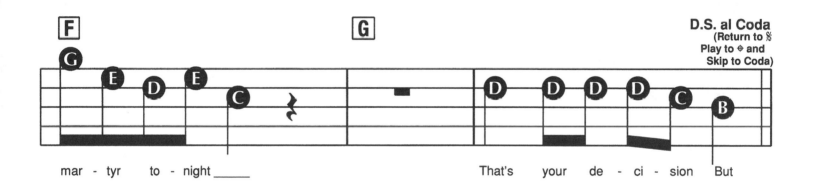

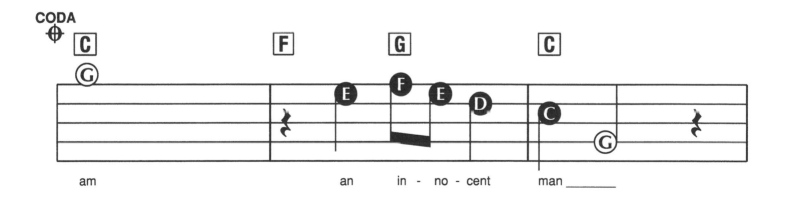

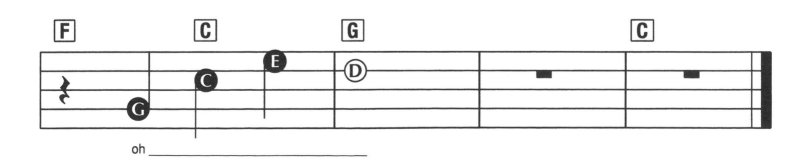

It's Still Rock And Roll To Me

Registration 2
Rhythm: Fox Trot or Swing

Words and Music by
Billy Joel

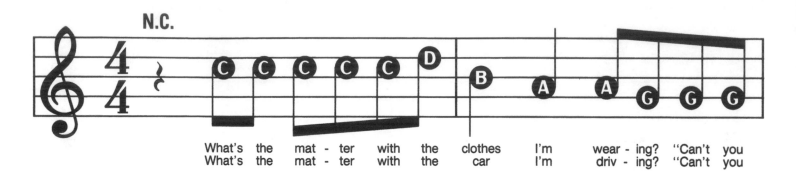

What's the mat - ter with the clothes I'm wear - ing? "Can't you
What's the mat - ter with the car I'm driv - ing? "Can't you

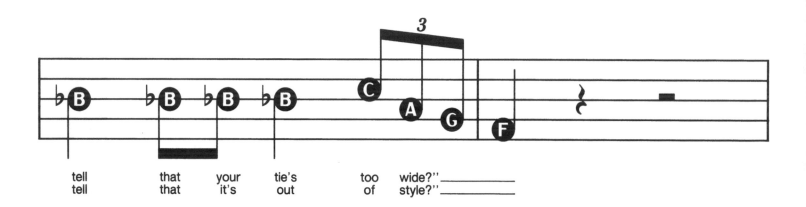

tell that your tie's too wide?"_____
tell that it's out of style?"_____

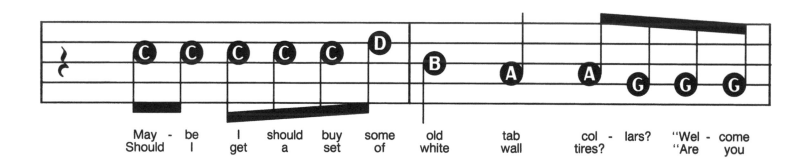

May - be I should buy some old tab col - lars? "Wel - come
Should I get a buy set some of white wall tires? "Are you

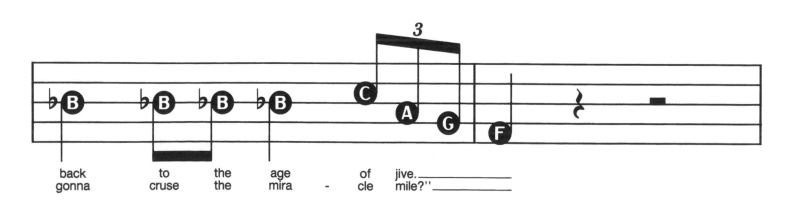

back to the age of jive._____
gonna cruse the mira - cle mile?"_____

© 1980 IMPULSIVE MUSIC
All Rights Controlled and Administered by EMI APRIL MUSIC INC.
All Rights Reserved   International Copyright Secured   Used by Permission

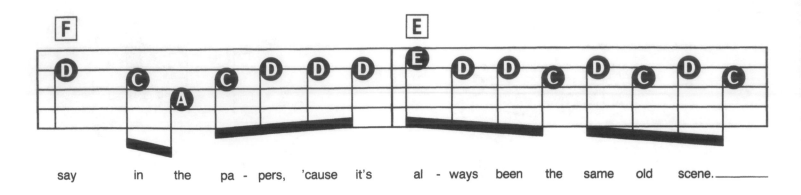

say   in the pa - pers, 'cause it's al - ways been the same old scene.____

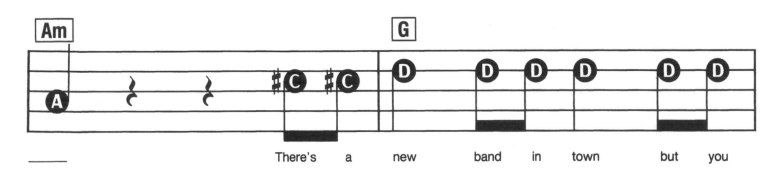

____   There's a new band in town but you

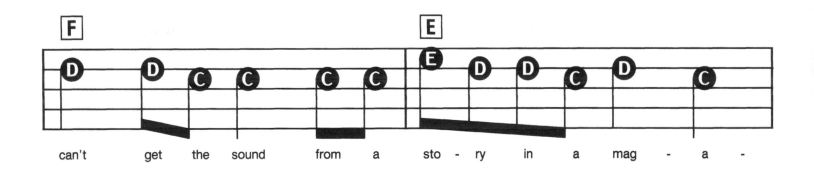

can't get the sound from a sto - ry in a mag - a -

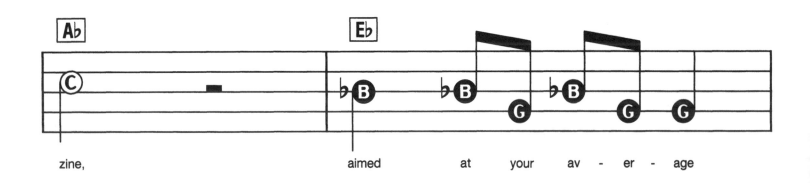

zine,   aimed at your av - er - age

teen.   How a - bout a pair of

     What's the mat - ter with the

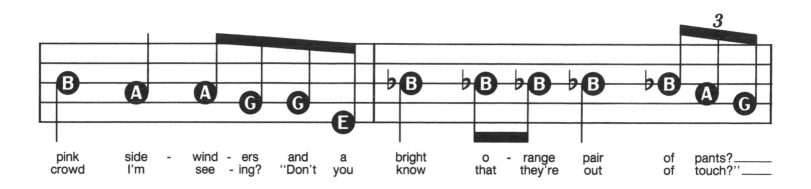

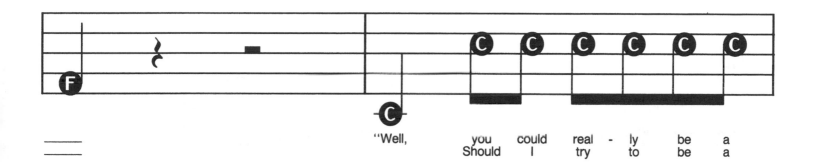

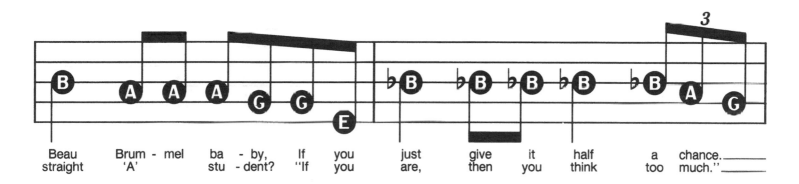

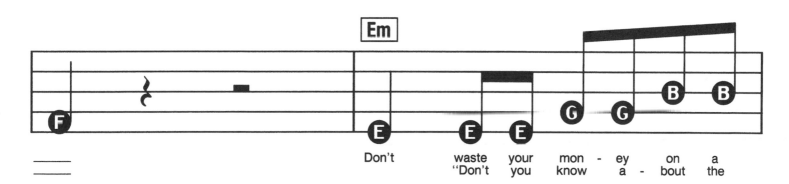

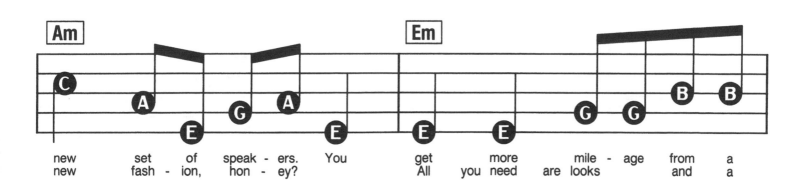

23

24

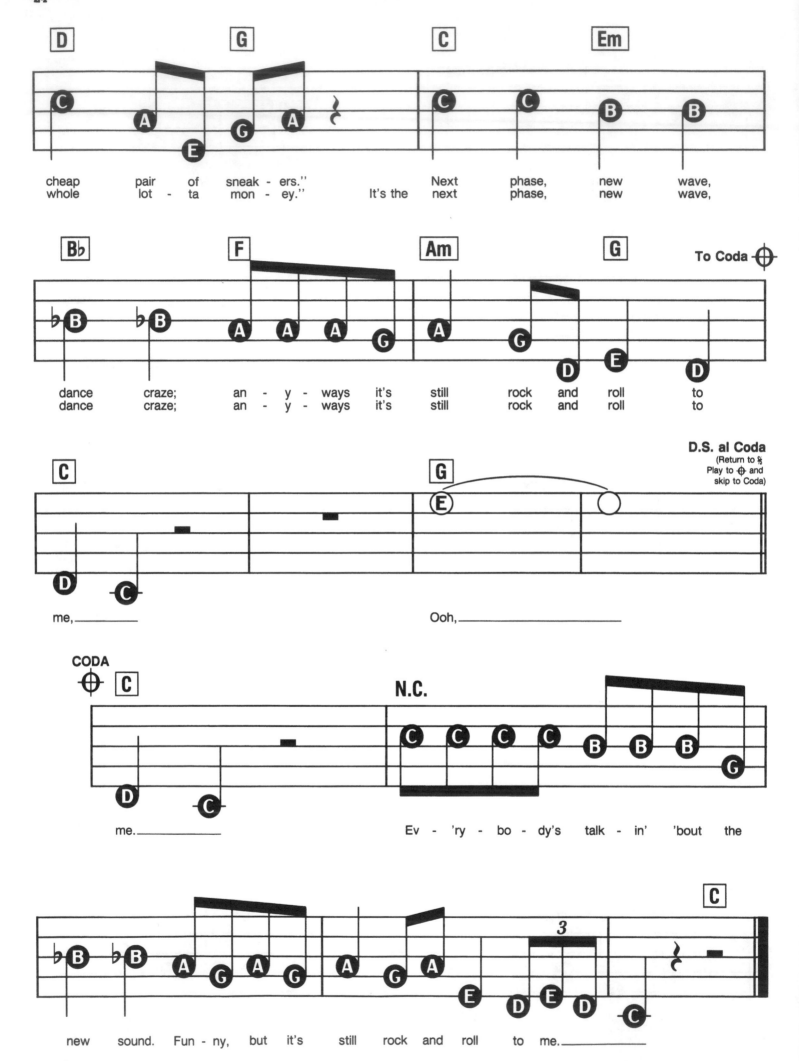

Allentown

Registration 1
Rhythm: Rock

Words and Music by
Billy Joel

© 1981, 1982 JOEL SONGS
All Rights Controlled and Administered by EMI BLACKWOOD MUSIC INC.
All Rights Reserved   International Copyright Secured

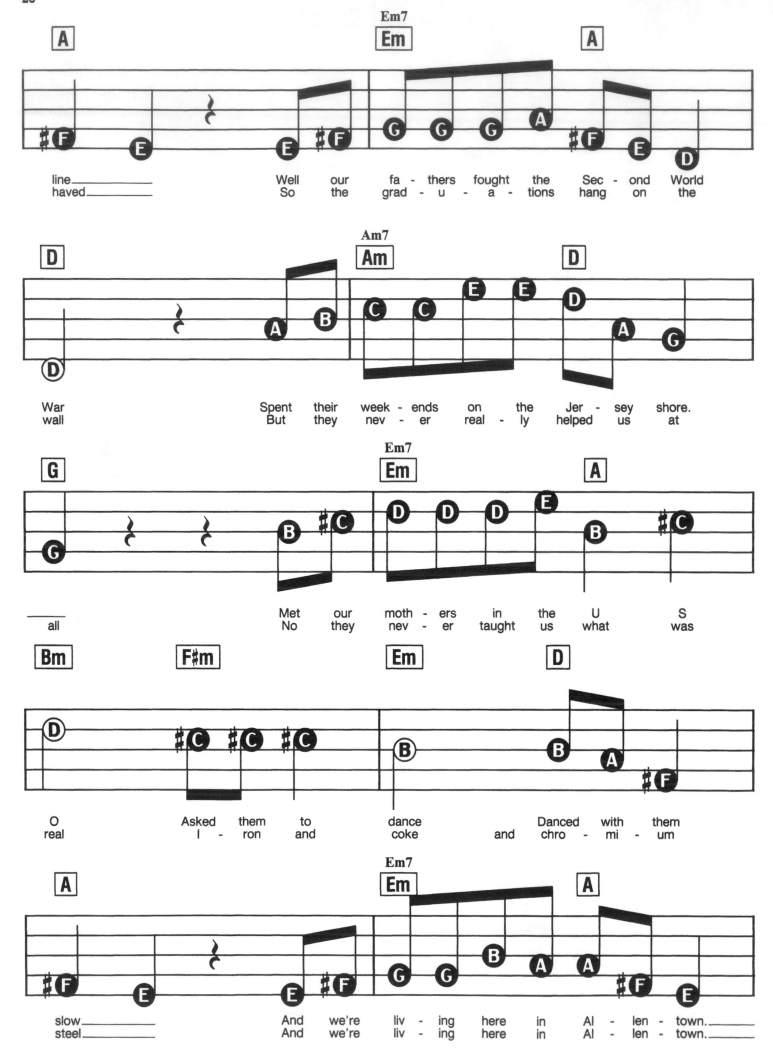

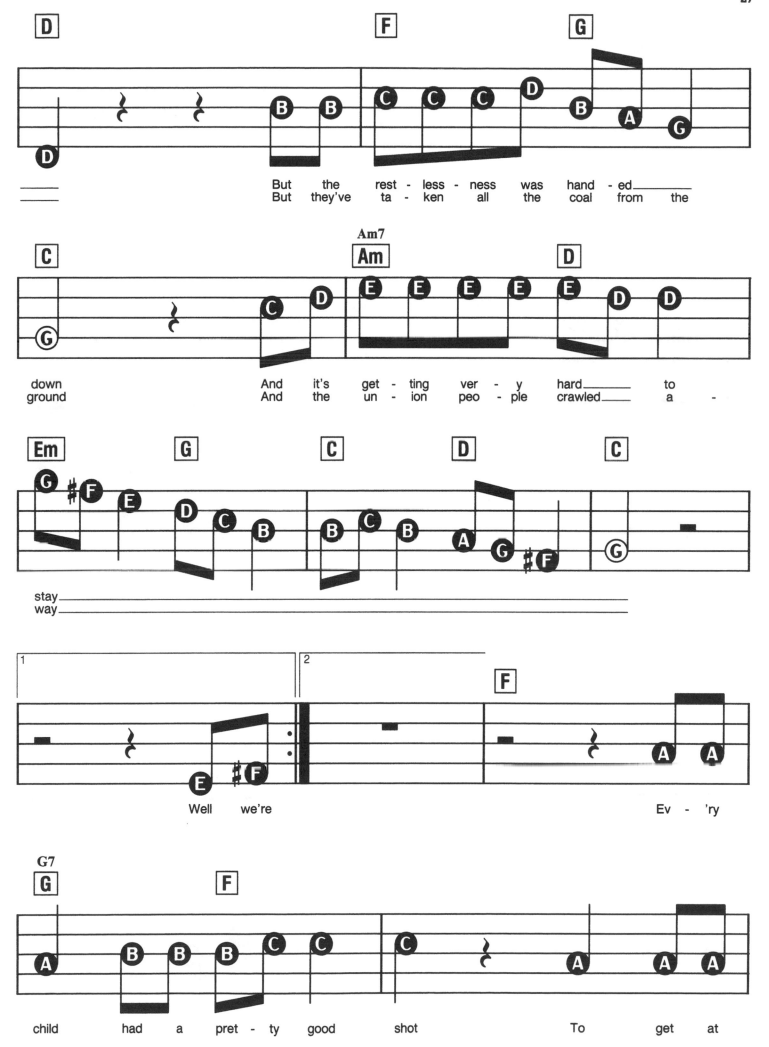

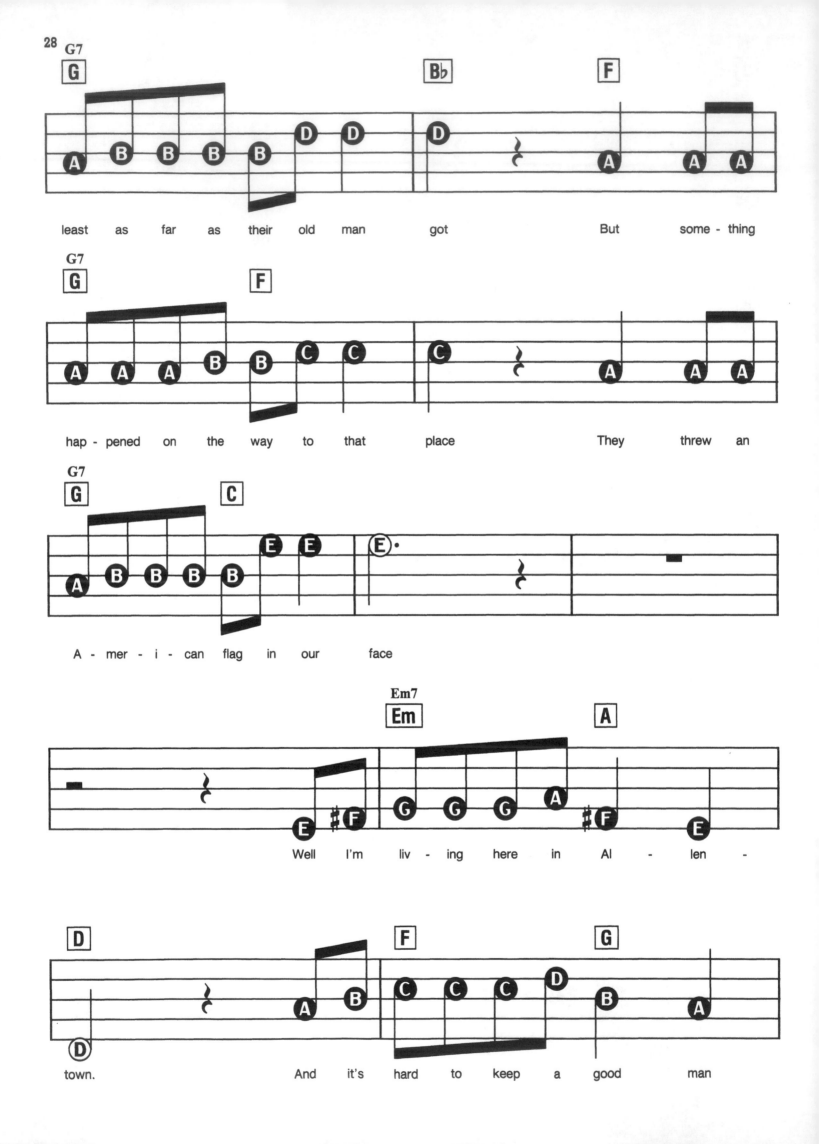

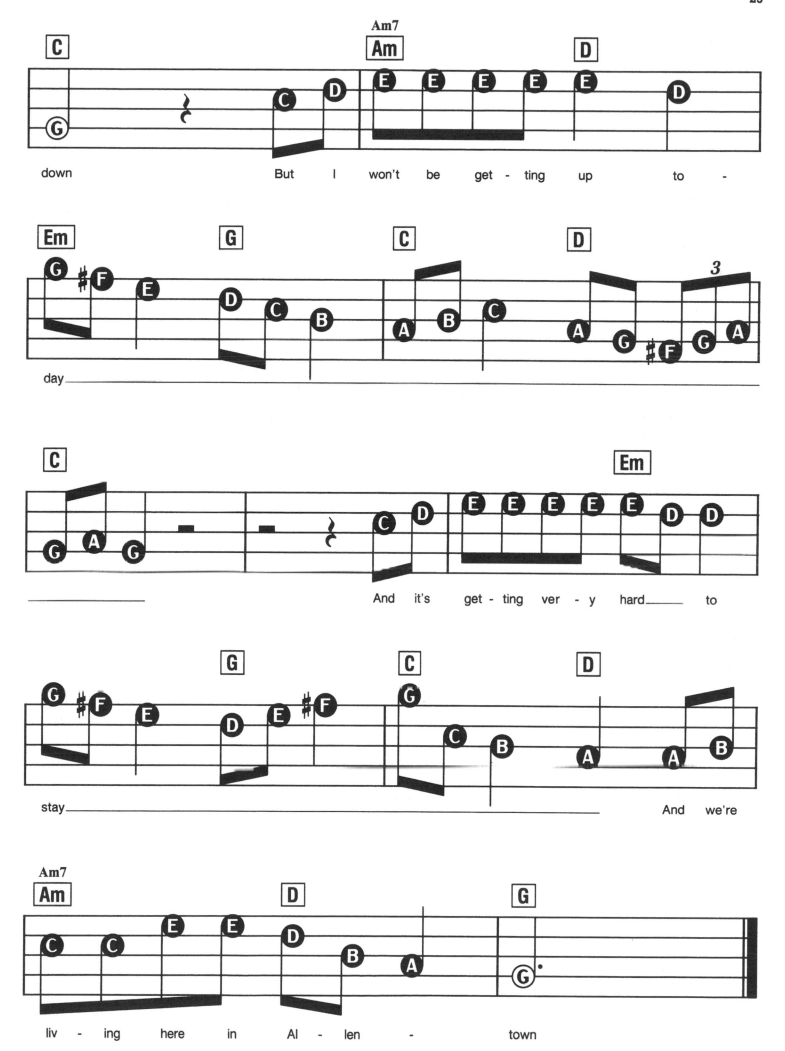

Just The Way You Are

Registration 4
Rhythm: Rock or Jazz Rock

Words and Music by
Billy Joel

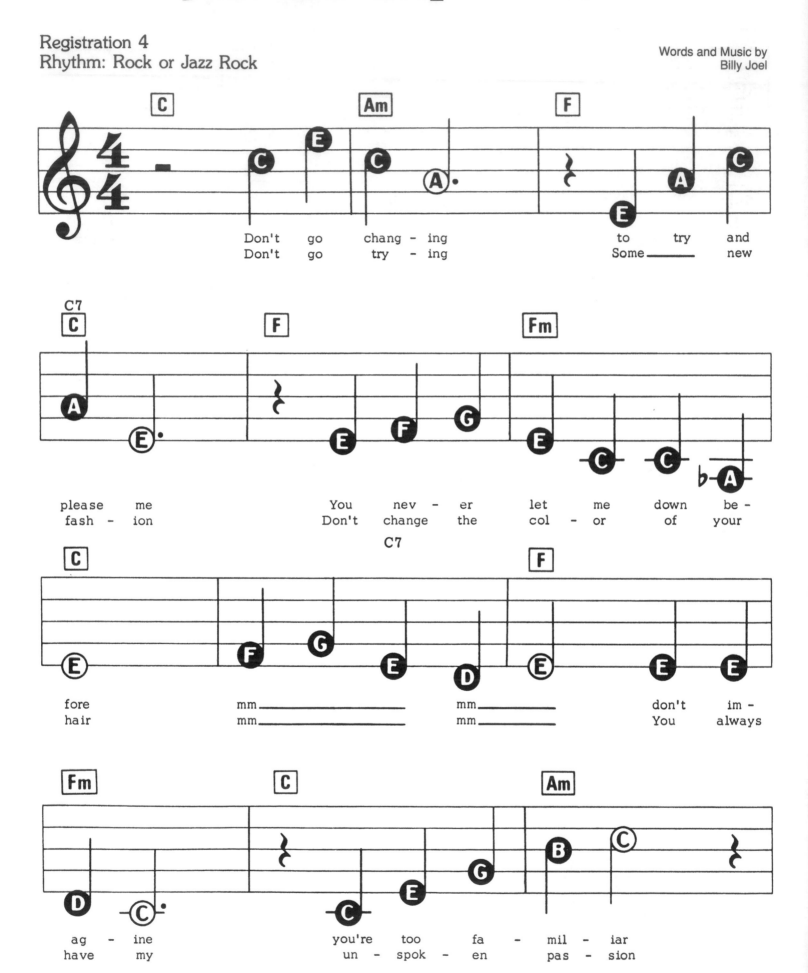

© 1977, 1978 IMPULSIVE MUSIC
All Rights Controlled and Administered by EMI APRIL MUSIC INC.
All Rights Reserved   International Copyright Secured   Used by Permission

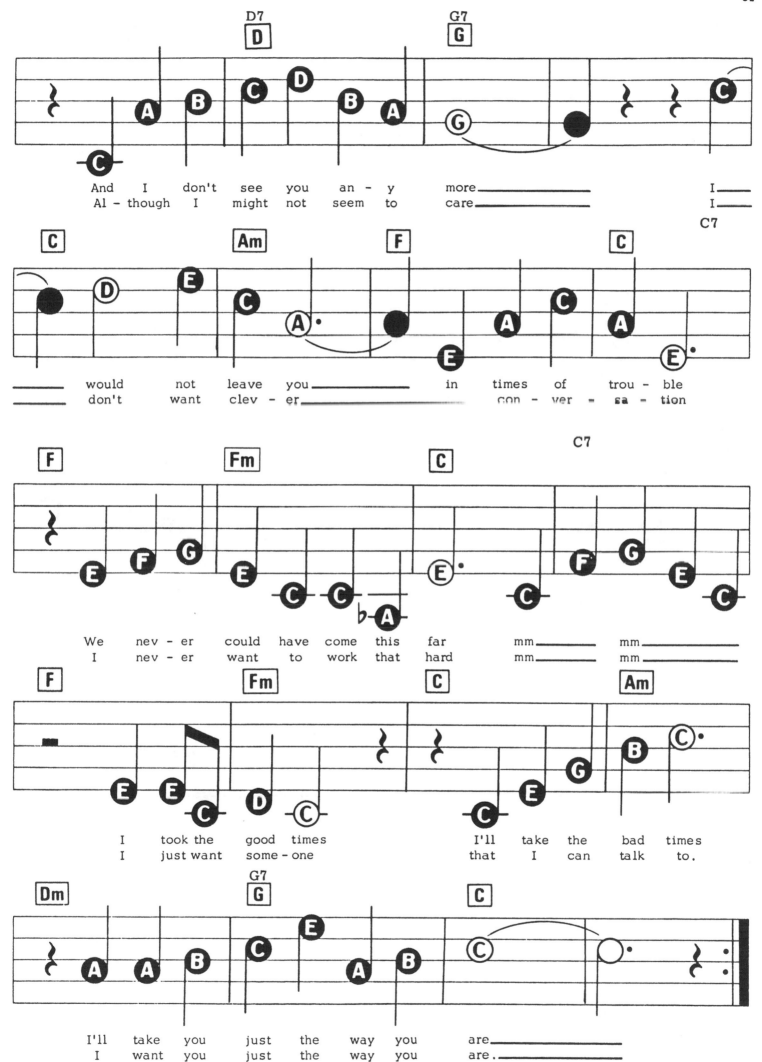

32

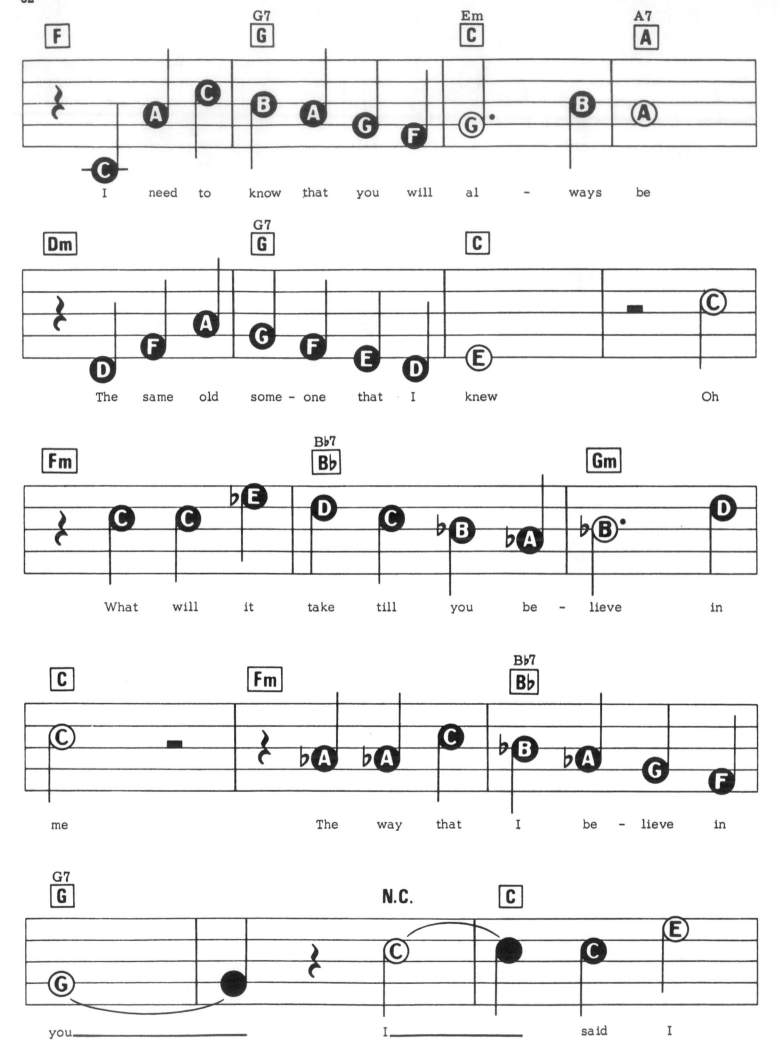

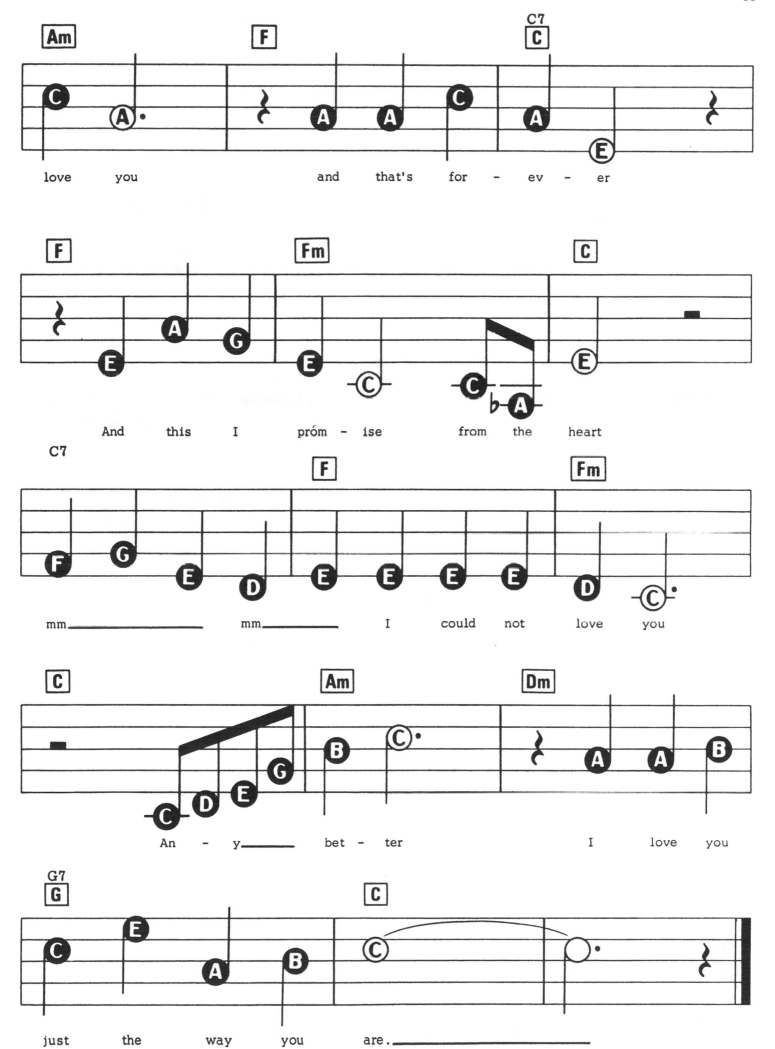

Keeping The Faith

Registration 2
Rhythm: March

Words and Music by
Billy Joel

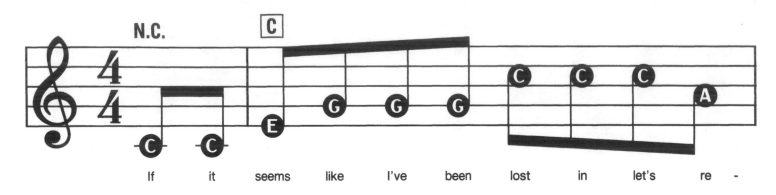

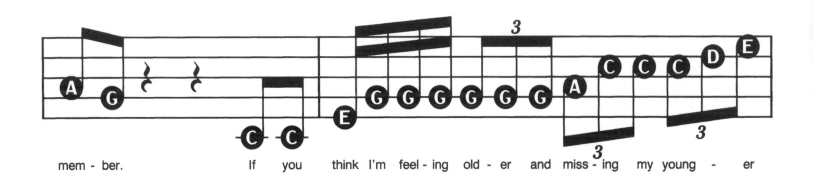

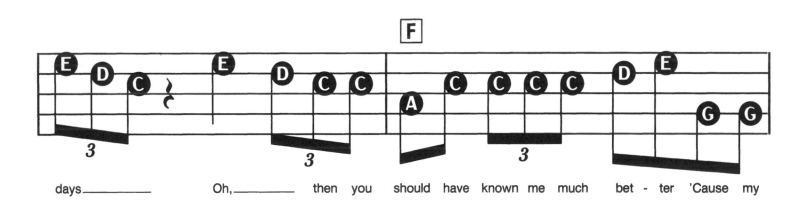

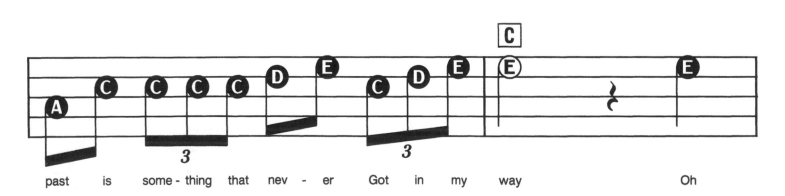

© 1983 JOEL SONGS
All Rights Controlled and Administered by EMI BLACKWOOD MUSIC INC.
All Rights Reserved   International Copyright Secured   Used by Permission

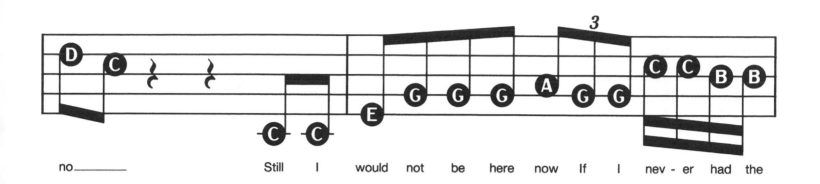

no_____ Still I would not be here now If I nev - er had the

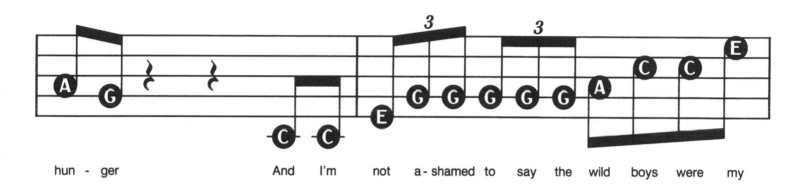

hun - ger And I'm not a - shamed to say the wild boys were my

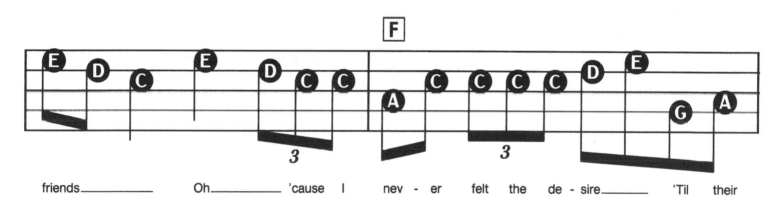

friends_____ Oh_____ 'cause I nev - er felt the de - sire_____ 'Til their

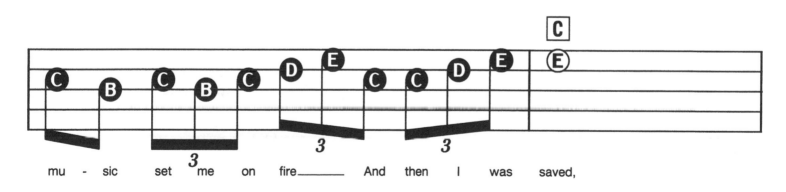

mu - sic set me on fire_____ And then I was saved,

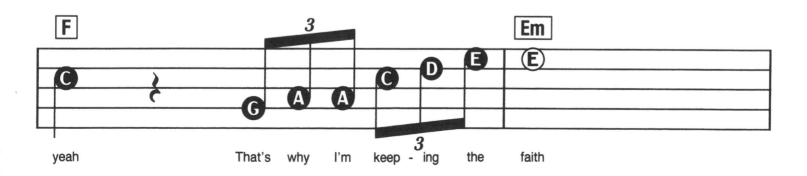

yeah That's why I'm keep - ing the faith

36

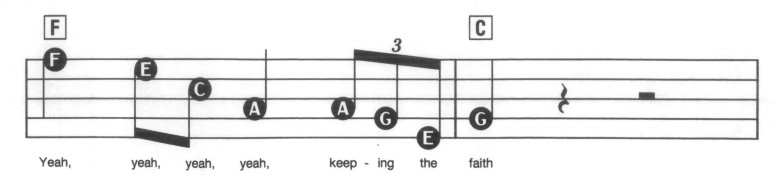

Yeah, yeah, yeah, yeah, keep - ing the faith

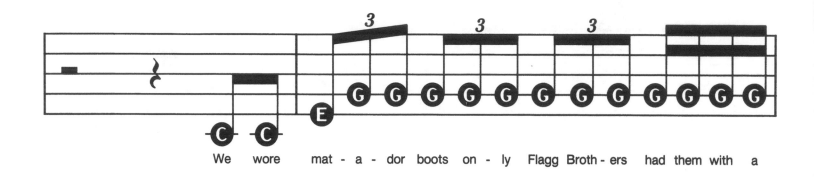

We wore mat - a - dor boots on - ly Flagg Broth - ers had them with a

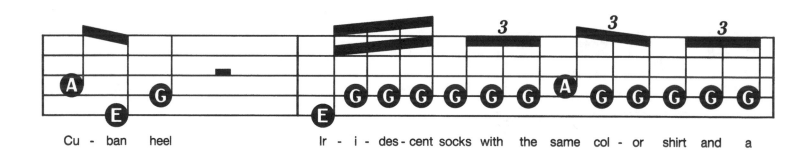

Cu - ban heel   Ir - i - des - cent socks with the same col - or shirt and a

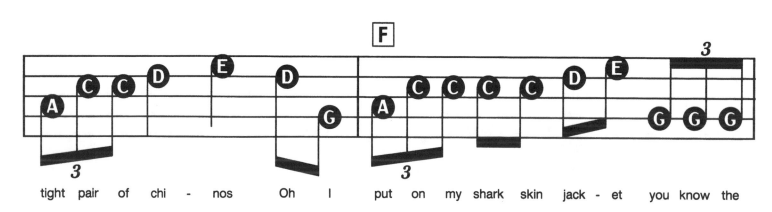

tight pair of chi - nos   Oh I put on my shark skin jack - et you know the

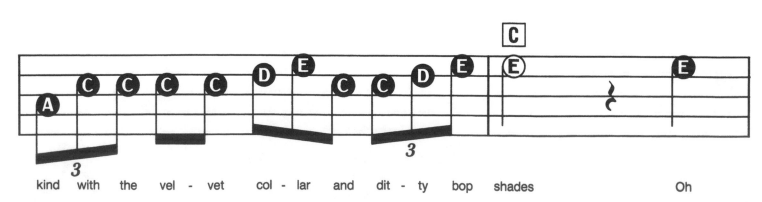

kind with the vel - vet col - lar and dit - ty bop shades   Oh

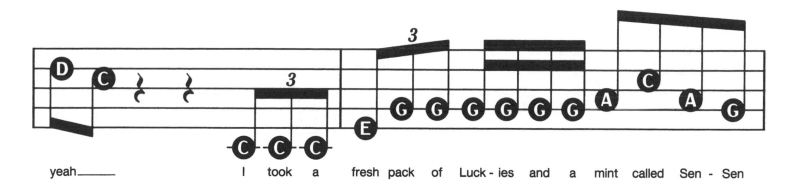

yeah_____ I took a fresh pack of Luck - ies and a mint called Sen - Sen

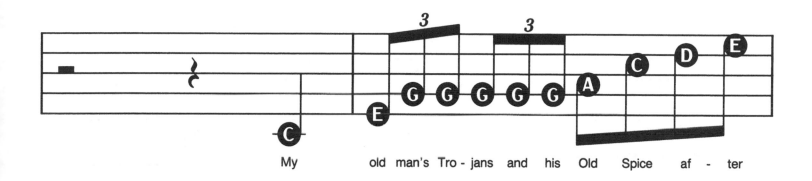

My old man's Tro - jans and his Old Spice af - ter

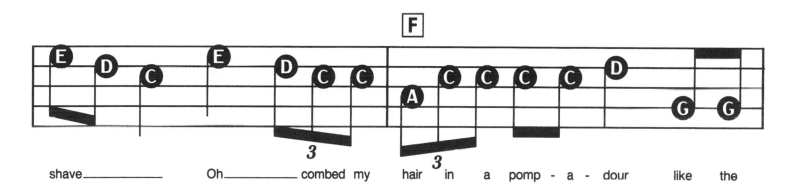

shave_____ Oh_____ combed my hair in a pomp - a - dour like the

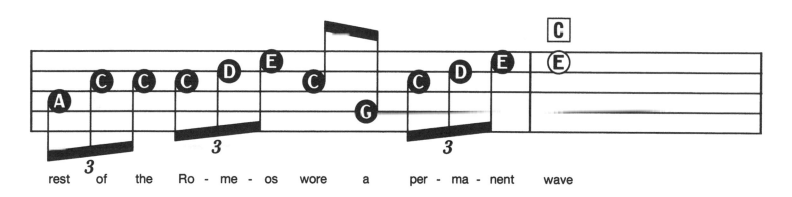

rest of the Ro - me - os wore a per - ma - nent wave

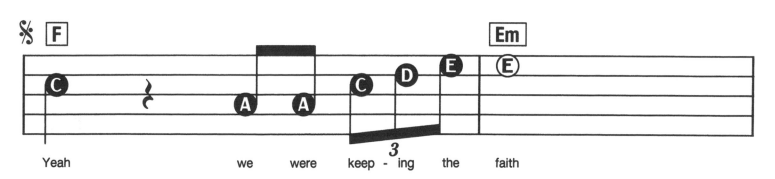

Yeah we were keep - ing the faith

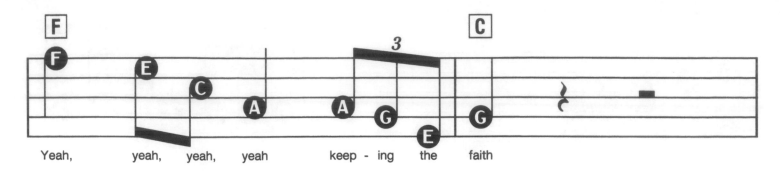

Yeah, yeah, yeah, yeah keep - ing the faith

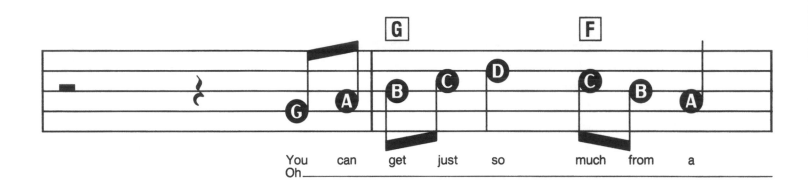

You can get just so much from a
Oh

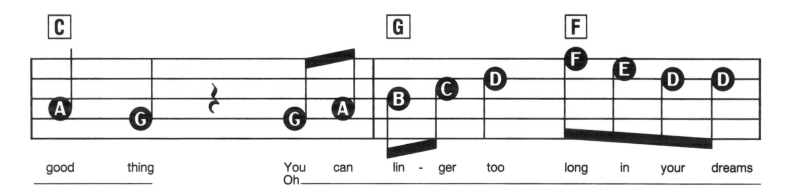

good thing You can lin - ger too long in your dreams
Oh

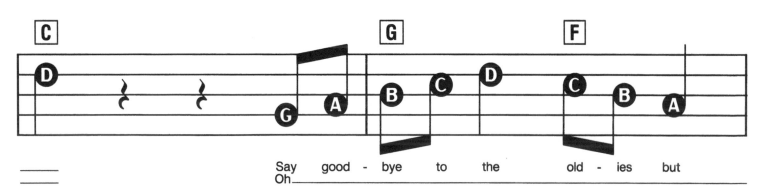

Say good - bye to the old - ies but
Oh

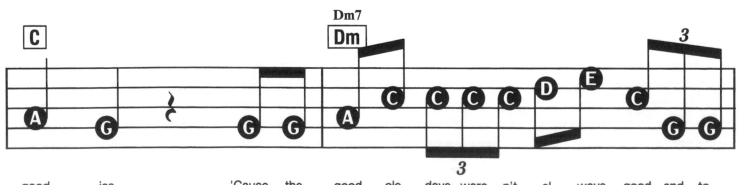

good - ies 'Cause the good ole days were - n't al - ways good and to -
You know the good ole days were - n't al - ways good and to -

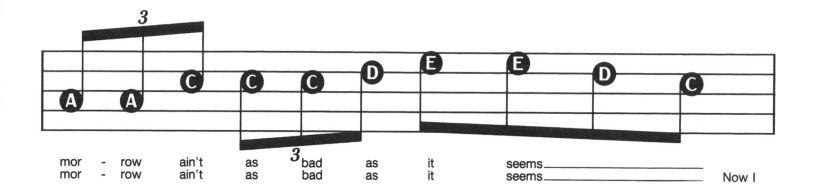

mor - row ain't as bad as it seems_____
mor - row ain't as bad as it seems_____ Now I

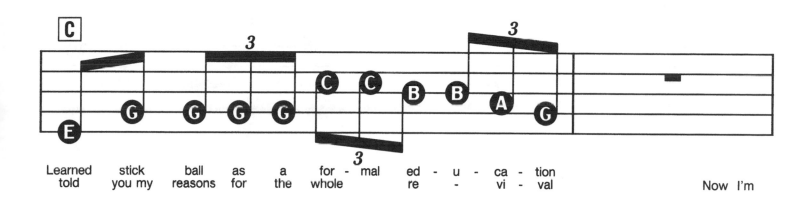

C

Learned stick ball as a for - mal ed - u - ca - tion
told you my reasons for the whole re - vi - val Now I'm

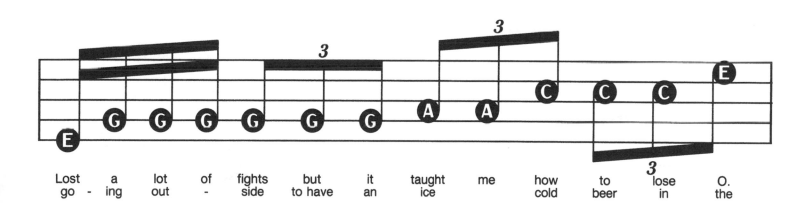

Lost a lot of fights but it taught me how to lose O.
go - ing out - side to have an ice cold beer in the

F   To Coda ⊕

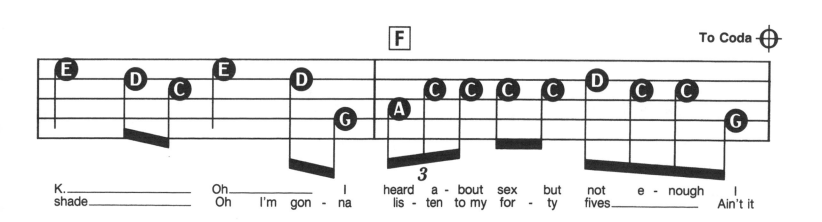

K._____ Oh_____ I heard a - bout sex but not e - nough I
shade_____ Oh I'm gon - na lis - ten to my for - ty fives_____ Ain't it

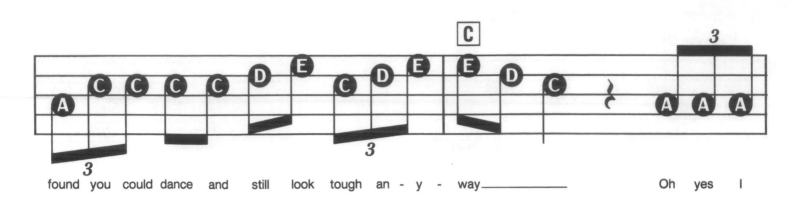

found you could dance and still look tough an-y-way_____ Oh yes I

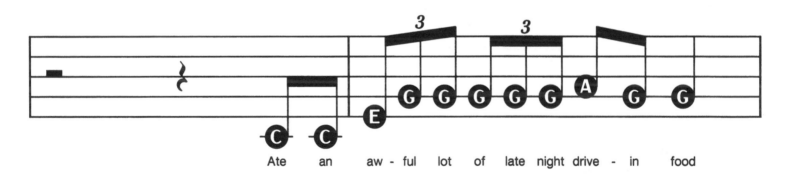

did_____ I found out a man ain't just be-ing ma-cho

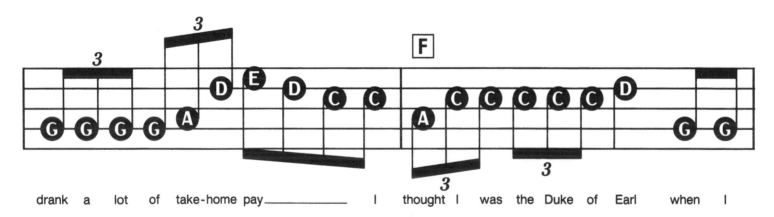

Ate an aw-ful lot of late night drive-in food

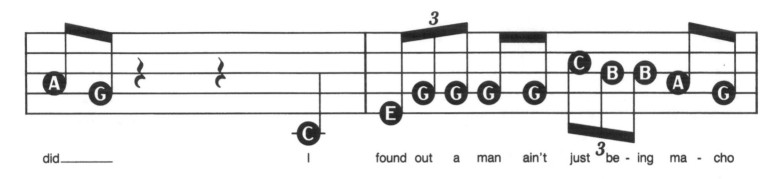

drank a lot of take-home pay_____ I thought I was the Duke of Earl when I

D.S. al Coda
(Return to 𝄋
Play to ⊕ and
skip to Coda)

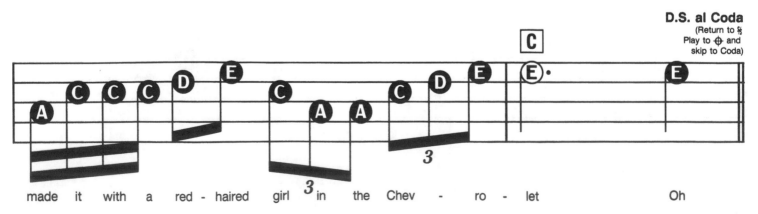

made it with a red-haired girl in the Chev-ro-let Oh

CODA

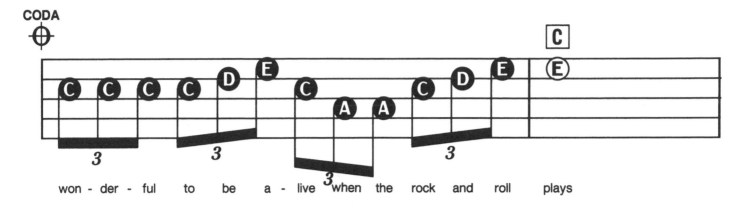

won - der - ful   to   be   a - live   when   the   rock   and   roll   plays

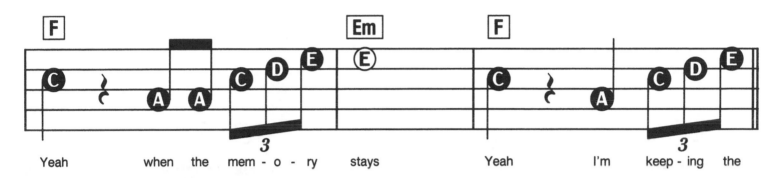

Yeah   when   the   mem - o - ry   stays   Yeah   I'm   keep - ing   the

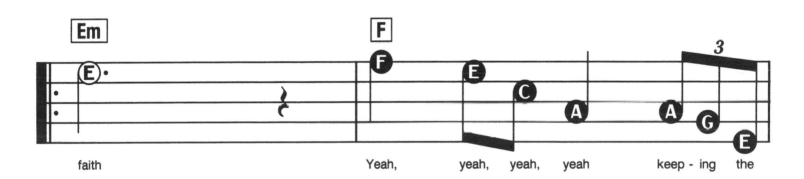

faith   Yeah,   yeah, yeah, yeah   keep - ing   the

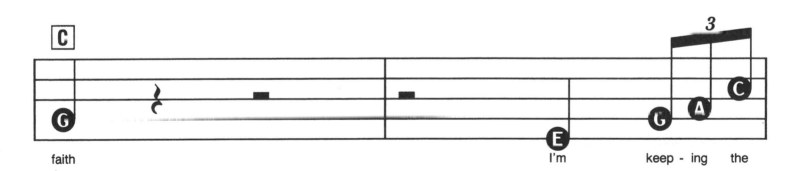

faith   I'm   keep - ing   the

Repeat and Fade

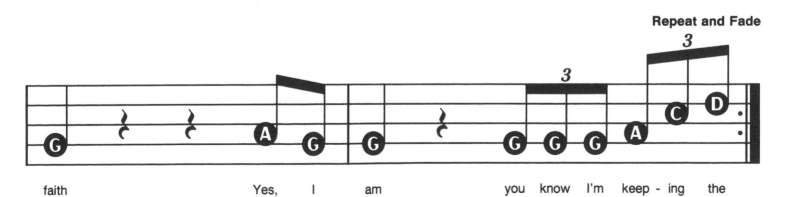

faith   Yes,   I   am   you know   I'm   keep - ing   the

The Longest Time

Registration 7
Rhythm: Rock

Words and Music by
Billy Joel

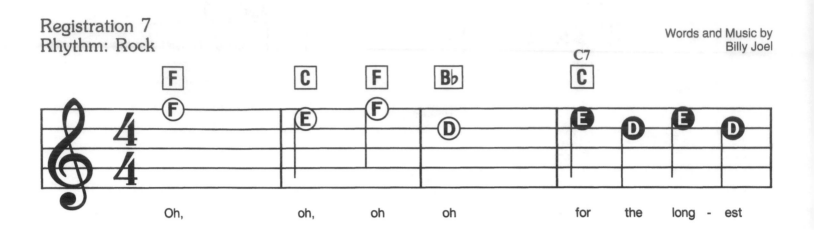

Oh,   oh,   oh   oh   for   the   long - est

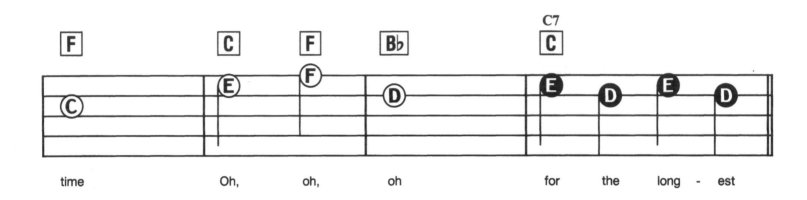

time   Oh,   oh,   oh   for   the   long - est

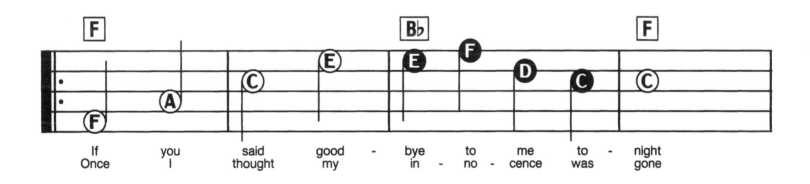

If   you   said   good - bye   to   me   to - night
Once   I   thought   my   in - no - cence   was   gone

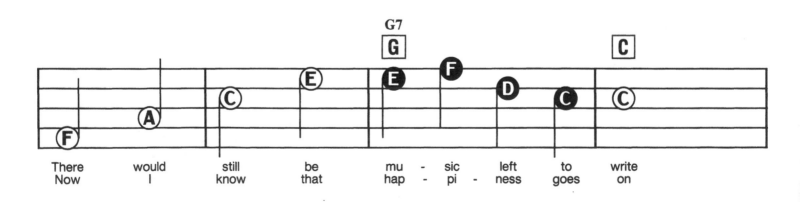

There   would   still   be   mu - sic   left   to   write
Now   I   know   that   hap - pi - ness   goes   on

© 1983 JOEL SONGS
All Rights Controlled and Administered by EMI BLACKWOOD MUSIC INC.
All Rights Reserved   International Copyright Secured   Used by Permission

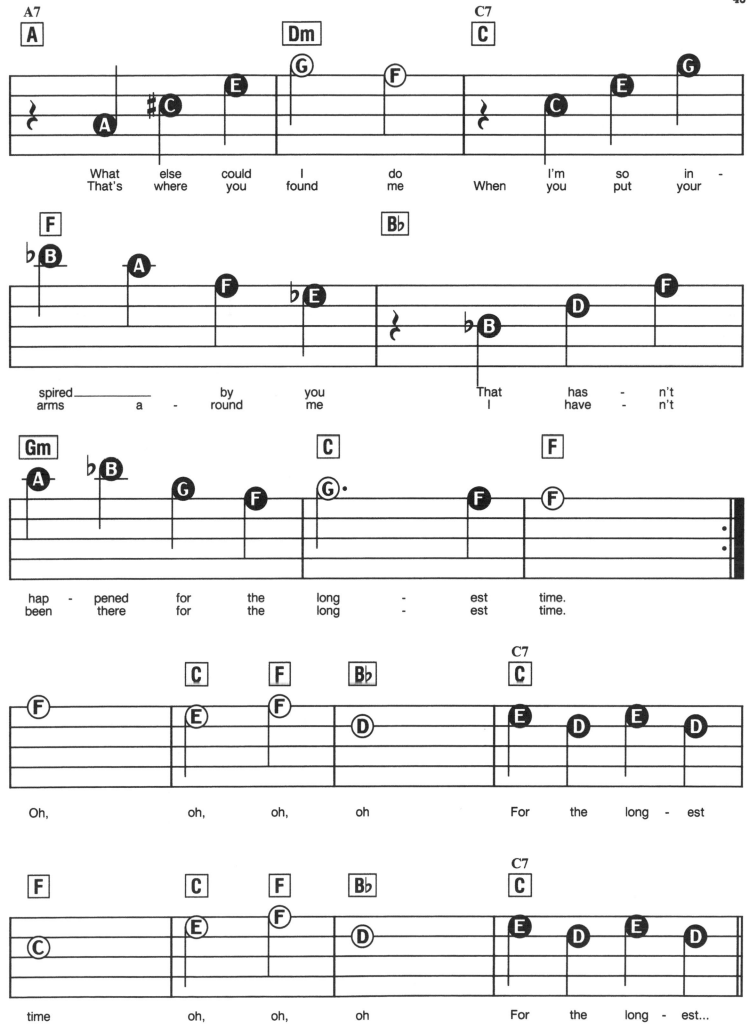

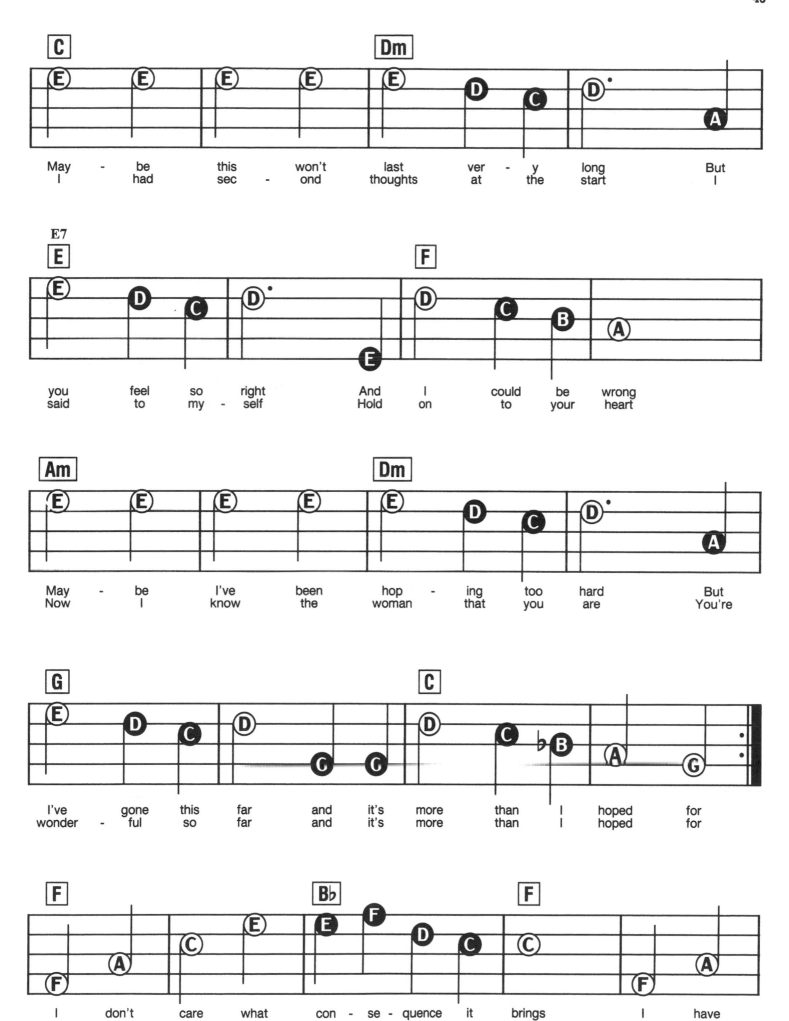

A Matter Of Trust

Registration 4
Rhythm: Rock

Words and Music by
Billy Joel

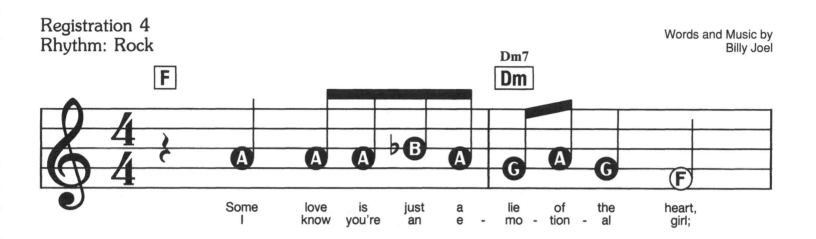

Some love is just a lie of the heart,
I know you're an e - mo - tion - al girl;

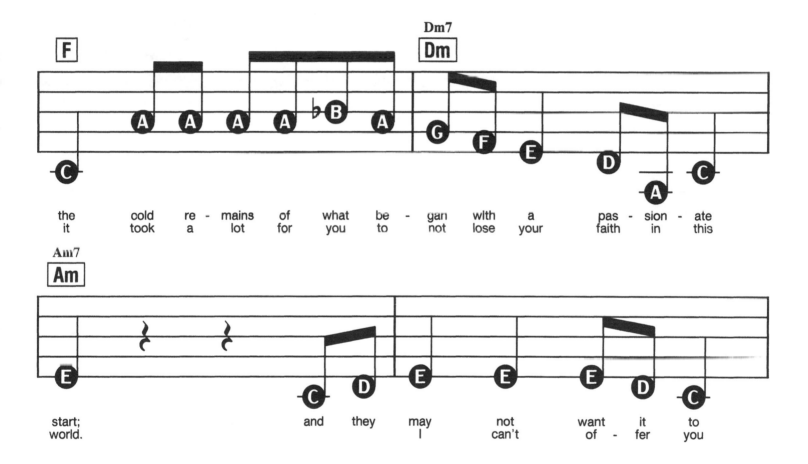

the cold re - mains of what be - gan with a pas - sion - ate
it took a lot for you to not lose your faith in this

start; and they may not want it to
world. I can't of - fer you

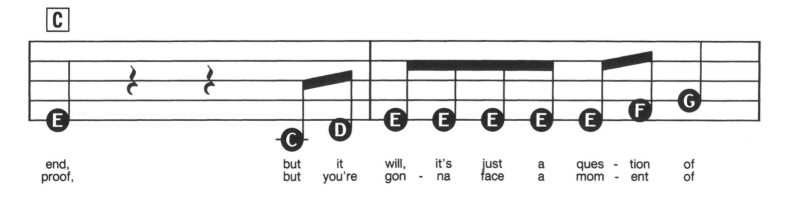

end, but it will, it's just a ques - tion of
proof, but you're gon - na face a mom - ent of

© 1986 JOEL SONGS
All Rights Controlled and Administered by EMI BLACKWOOD MUSIC INC.
All Rights Reserved   International Copyright Secured   Used by Permission

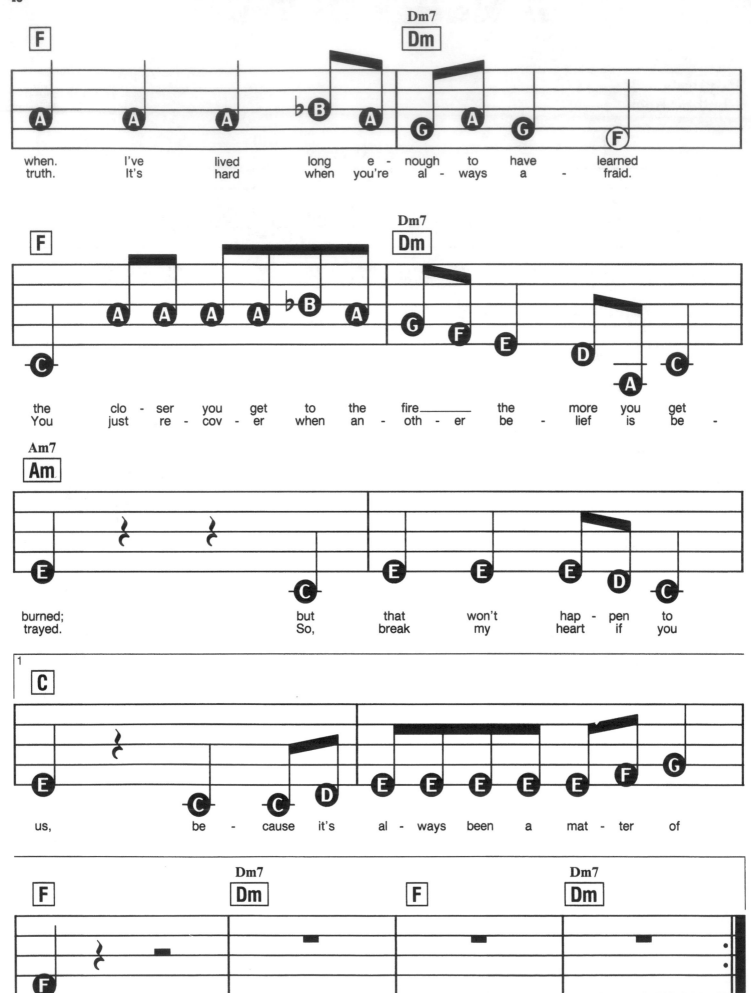

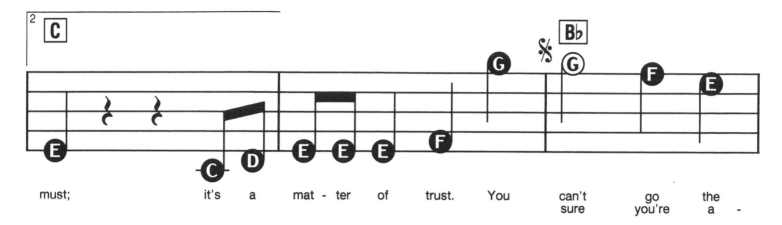

must; it's a mat-ter of trust. You can't go the
sure you're a -

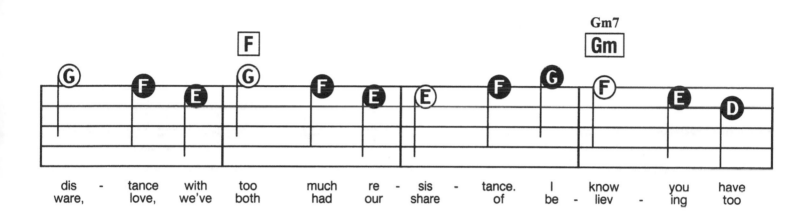

dis - tance with too much re - sis - tance. I know you have
ware, love, we've both had our share of be - liev - ing have too

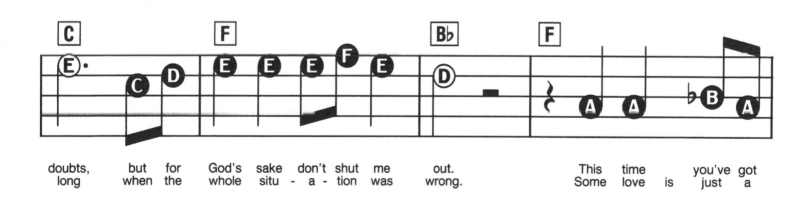

doubts, but for God's sake don't shut me out. This time you've got
long when the whole situ - a - tion was wrong. Some love is just a

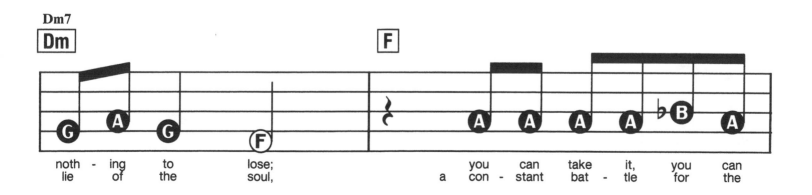

noth - ing to lose; you can take it, you can
lie of to the soul, a con - stant bat - tle you for the

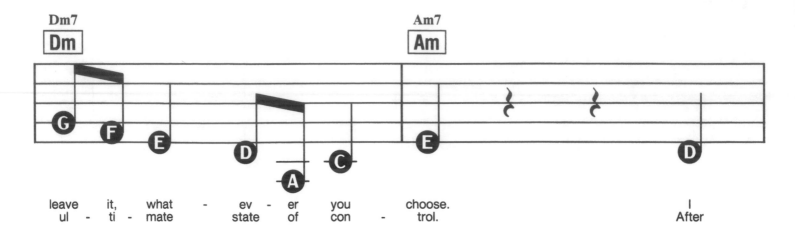

Dm7 / Dm / Am7 / Am

leave it, what - ev - er you choose. I
ul - ti - mate state of con - trol. After

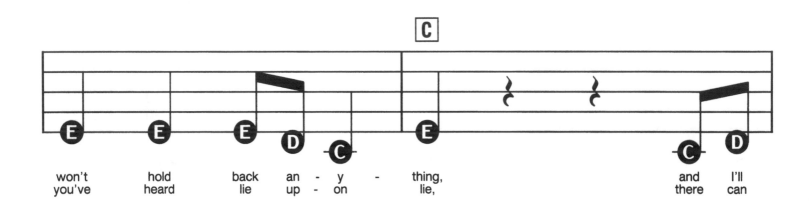

C

won't hold back an - y - thing, and I'll
you've heard lie up - on lie, there can

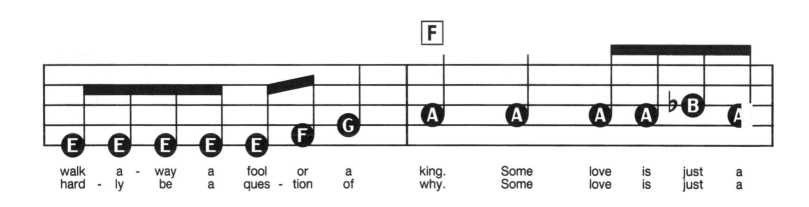

F

walk a - way a fool or a king. Some love is just a
hard - ly be a ques - tion of why. Some love is just a

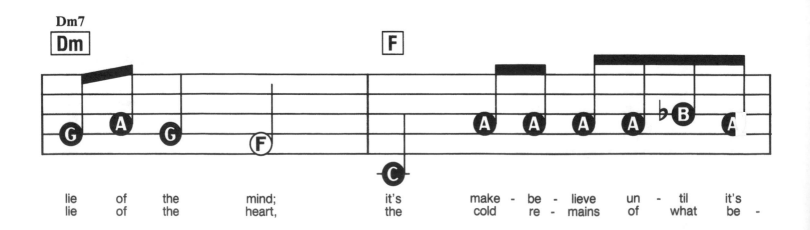

Dm7 / Dm / F

lie of the mind; it's the make - be - lieve un - til it's
lie of the heart, the cold re - mains of what be -

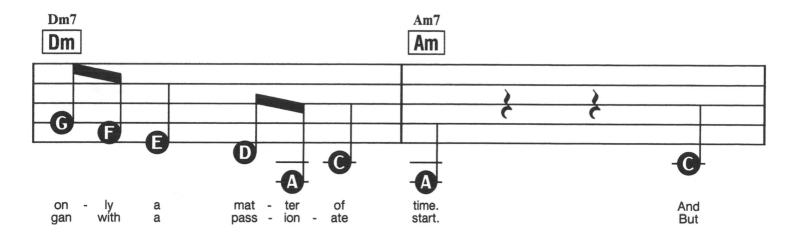

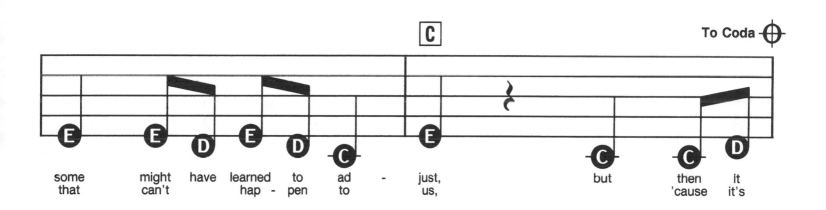

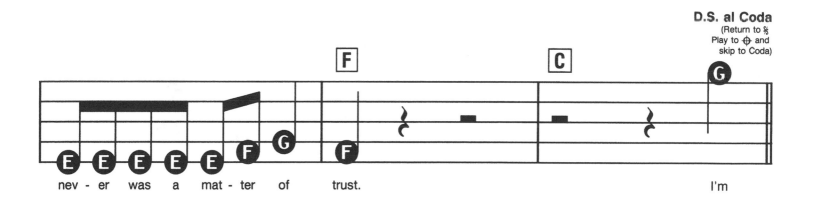

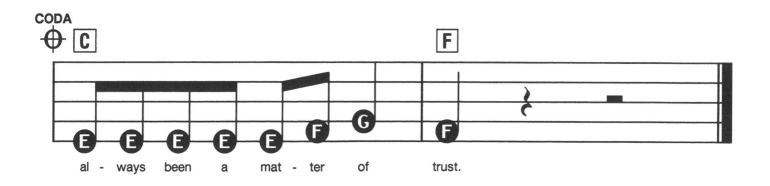

Modern Woman

Registration 7
Rhythm: Rock or 8 Beat

Words and Music by
Billy Joel

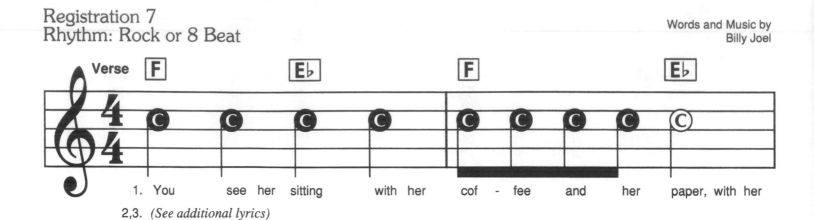

1. You see her sitting with her cof - fee and her paper, with her

2,3. *(See additional lyrics)*

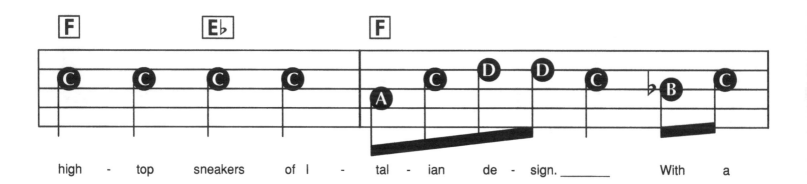

high - top sneakers of I - tal - ian de - sign. _____ With a

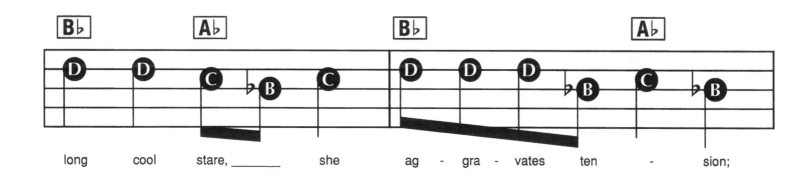

long cool stare, _____ she ag - gra - vates ten - sion;

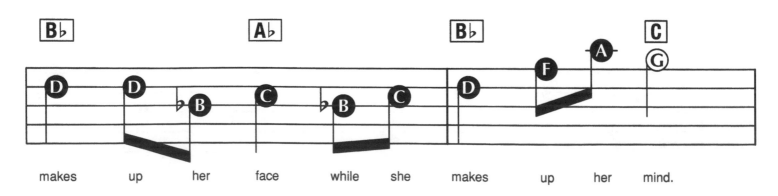

makes up her face while she makes up her mind.

© 1986 JOEL SONGS
This arrangement Copyright © 1991 JOEL SONGS
All Rights Reserved and Administered by EMI BLACKWOOD MUSIC INC
All Rights Reserved   International Copyright Secured   Used by Permission

53

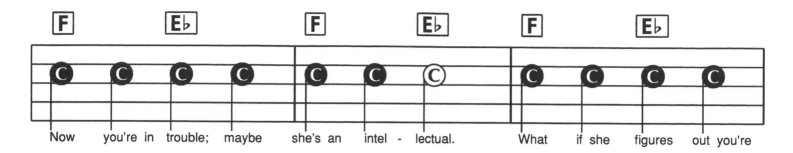

Now you're in trouble; maybe she's an intel - lectual. What if she figures out you're

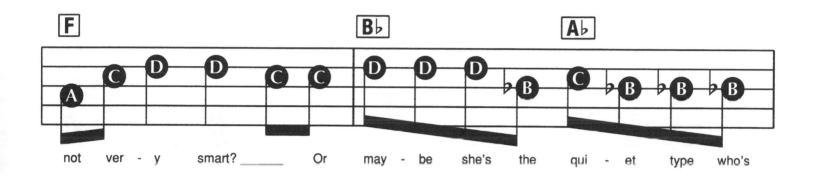

not ver - y smart? _____ Or may - be she's the qui - et type who's

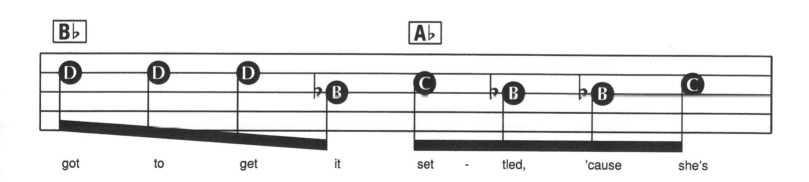

in - to heav - y met - al; boy, you

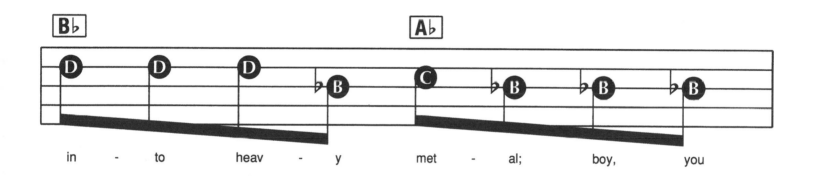

got to get it set - tled, 'cause she's

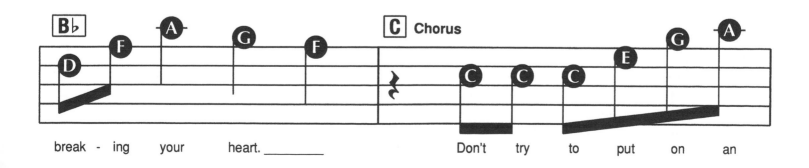

break - ing your heart. _____ Don't try to put on an

54

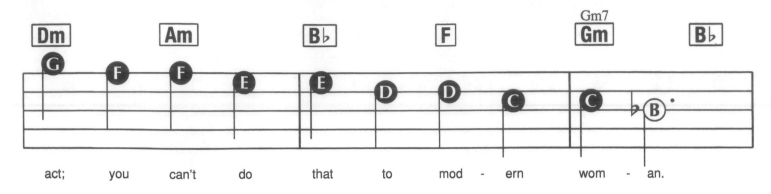

act; you can't do that to mod - ern wom - an.

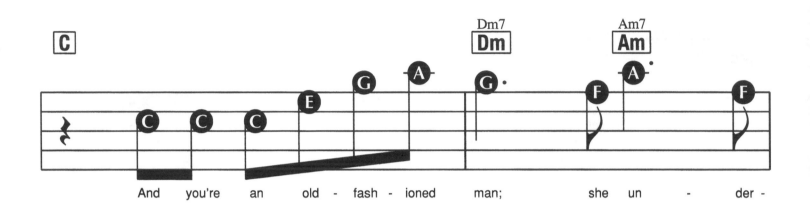

And you're an old - fash - ioned man; she un - der -

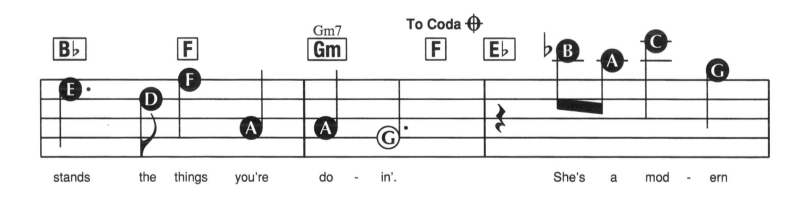

stands the things you're do - in'. She's a mod - ern

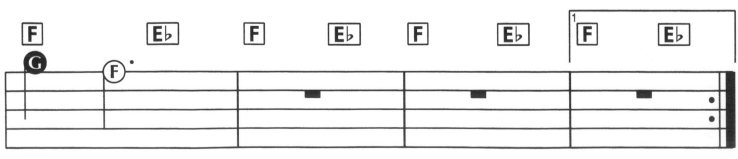

wom - an.

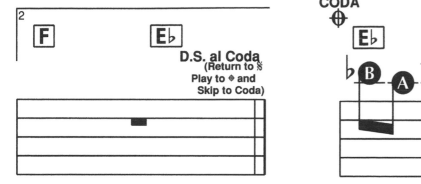

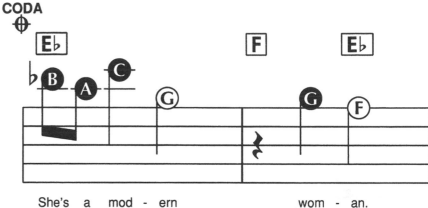

She's a mod - ern wom - an.

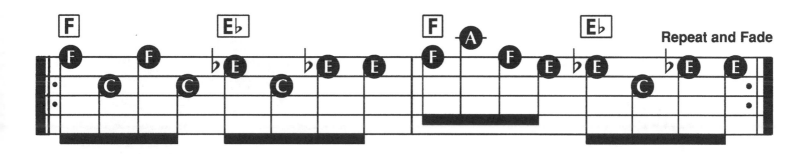

Repeat and Fade

Additional Lyrics

Verse 2:

She looks sleek and she seems so professional;
She's got a lot of confidence it's easy to see.
You want to make a move, but you feel so inferior
'Cause under that exterior is someone who's free.
She's got style and she's got her own money,
So she's not another honey you can quickly disarm.
She's got the eyes that make you realize
She won't be hypnotized by your usual charm.

Verse 3:

Time goes by, and you're sharing an apartment.
She says she loves you but she doesn't know why.
In the morning, she leaves you with your coffee and your paper;
It's a strange situation for an old-fashioned guy.
But times have changed; things are not the same, baby.
You overcame such a bad attitude.
Rock 'n' roll just used to be for kicks,
And nowadays it's politics,
And after 1986 what else could be new?

Chorus 2:

You've got your plan of attack;
That won't attract the modern woman.
When you're an old-fashioned man,
She understands the things you're doin'.
She's a modern woman.

Chorus 3:

You've got to learn to relax
And face the facts of modern woman.
And you're an old-fashioned man;
She understands the things you're doin'.
She's a modern woman.

My Life

Registration 2
Rhythm: Rock

Words and Music by
Billy Joel

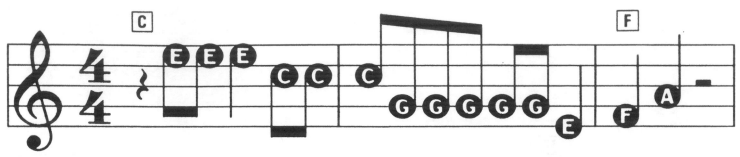

Got a call from an old ____ friend we used to be real close.
I don't need you to wor - ry for me ____ 'cause I'm al - right.

Said he could - n't go on the A - mer - i - can
I don't want you to tell me it's time to come

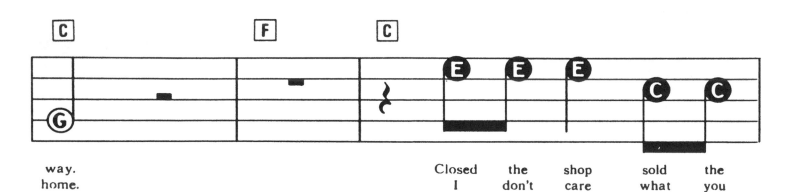

way.
home.

Closed the shop sold the
I don't care what you

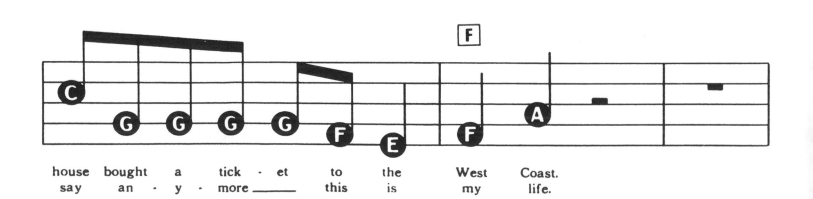

house bought a tick - et to the West Coast.
say an - y - more ____ this is my life.

© 1978 IMPULSIVE MUSIC
All Rights Controlled and Administered by EMI APRIL MUSIC INC.
All Rights Reserved   International Copyright Secured   Used by Permission

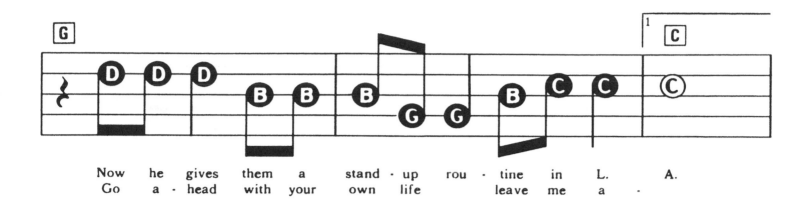

Now he gives them a stand - up rou - tine in L. A.
Go a - head with your own life leave me a -

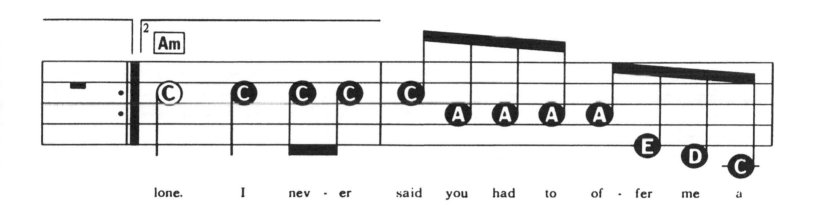

lone. I nev - er said you had to of - fer me a

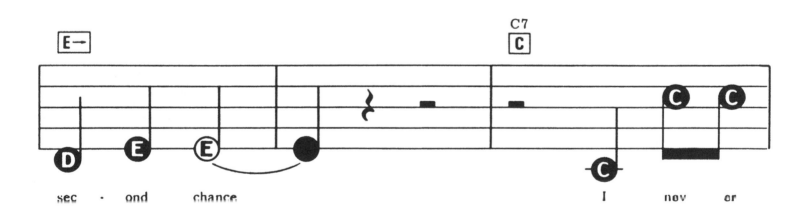

sec - ond chance I nev - er

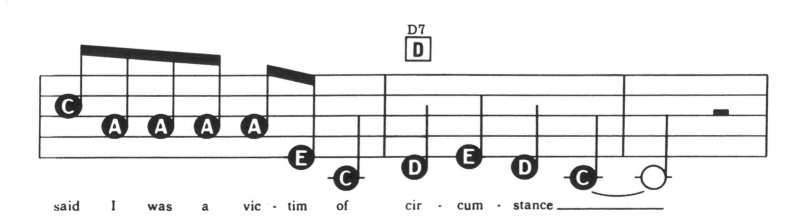

said I was a vic - tim of cir - cum - stance _____

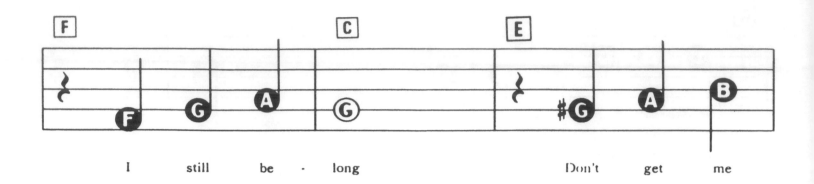

I still be - long   Don't get me

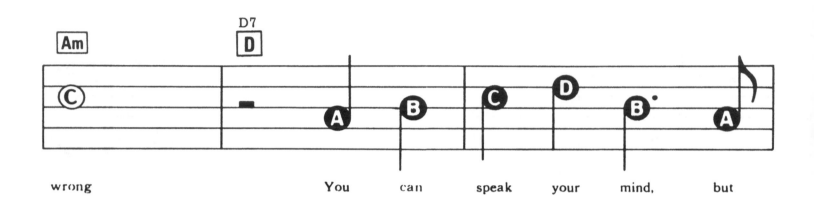

wrong   You can speak your mind, but

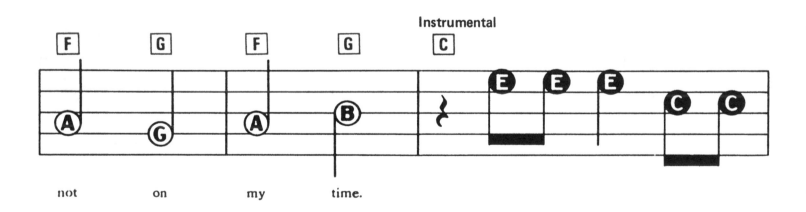

not   on   my   time.

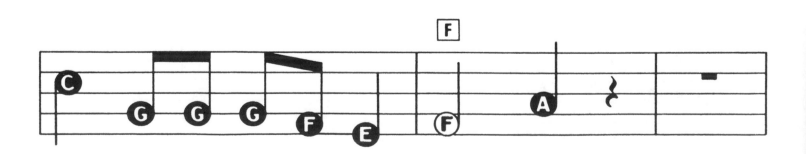

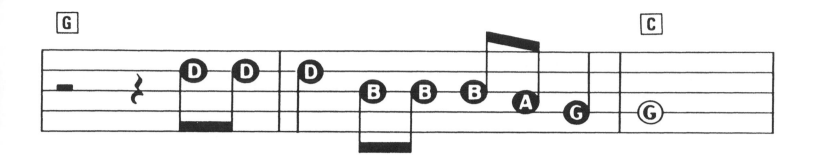

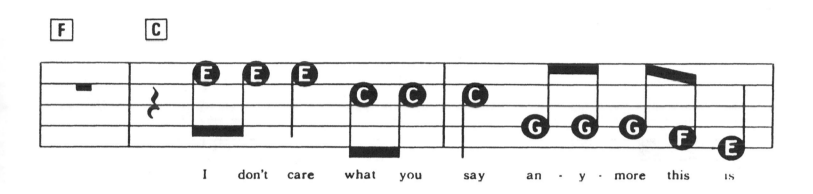

I don't care what you say an-y-more this is

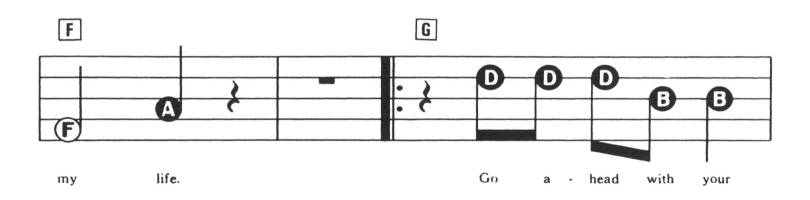

my life. Go a-head with your

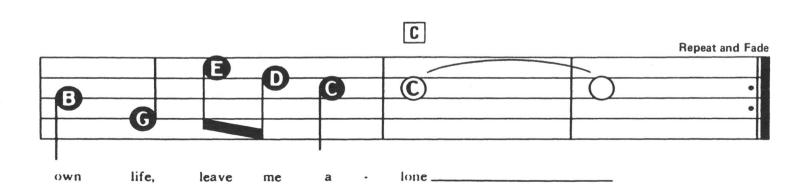

Repeat and Fade

own life, leave me a-lone _____

Only The Good Die Young

Registration 1
Rhythm: Rock

Words and Music by
Billy Joel

© 1977, 1978 IMPULSIVE MUSIC
All Rights Controlled and Administered by EMI APRIL MUSIC INC.
All Rights Reserved   International Copyright Secured   Used by Permission

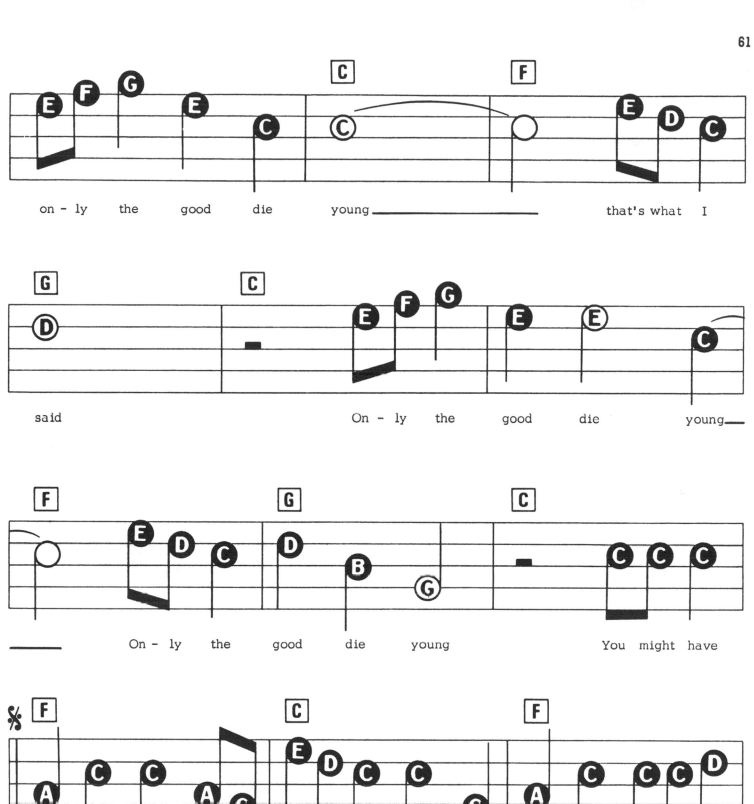

on - ly the good die young _____ that's what I

said On - ly the good die young___

On - ly the good die young You might have

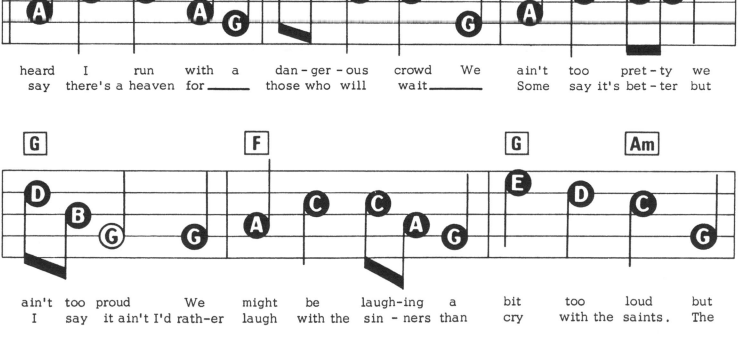

heard I run with a dan-ger-ous crowd We ain't too pret-ty we
say there's a heaven for___ those who will wait___ Some say it's bet-ter but

ain't too proud We might be laugh-ing a bit too loud but
I say it ain't I'd rath-er laugh with the sin-ners than cry with the saints. The

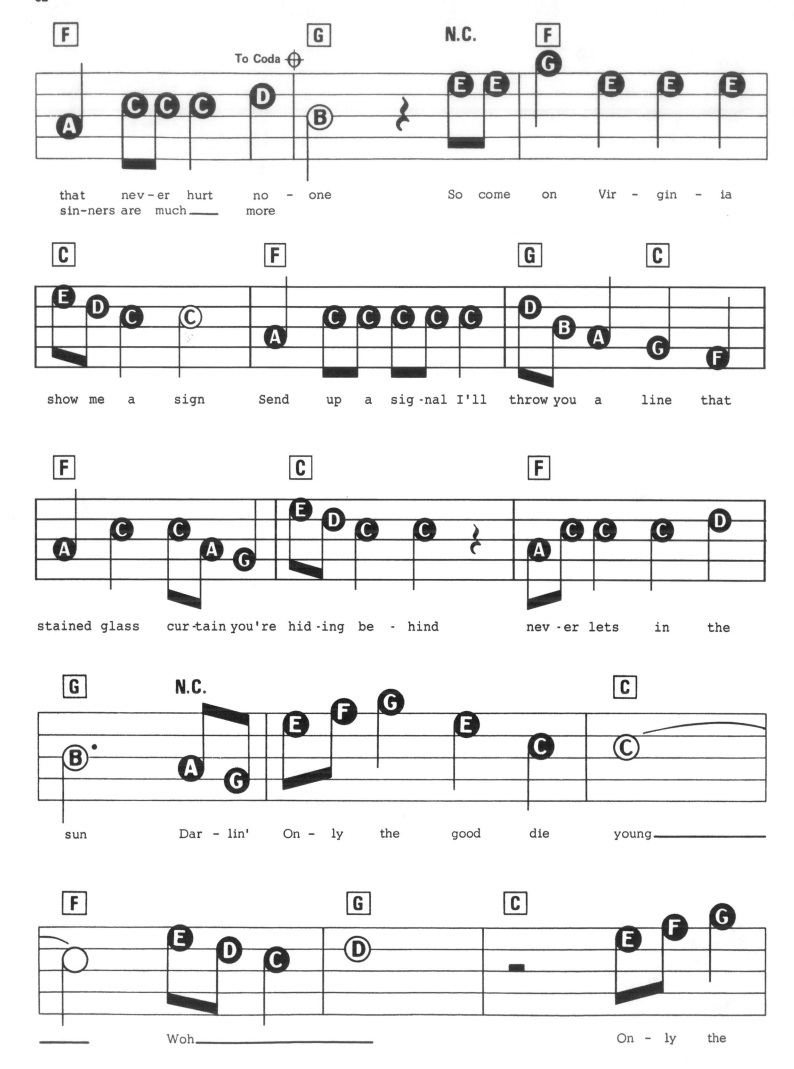

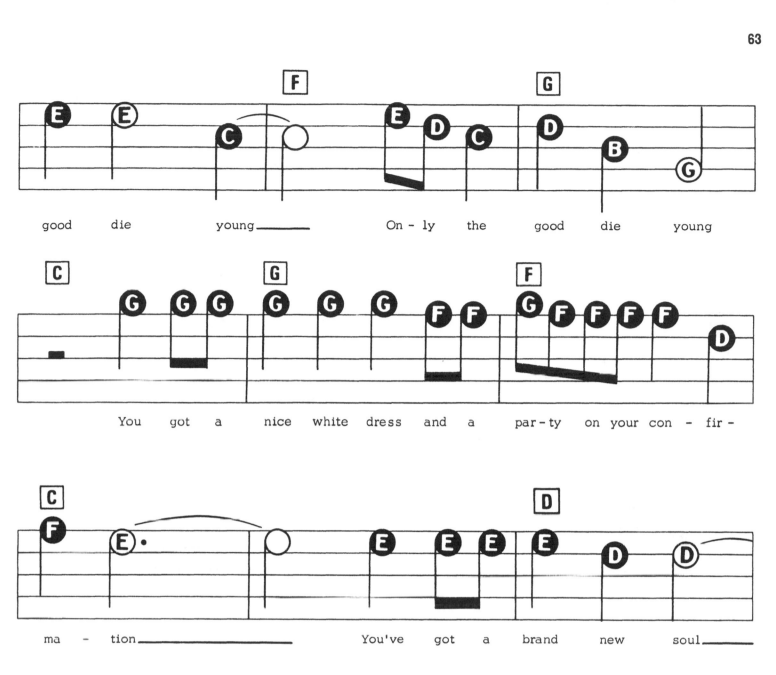

good die young_____ On - ly the good die young

You got a nice white dress and a par - ty on your con - fir -

ma - tion_____ You've got a brand new soul_____

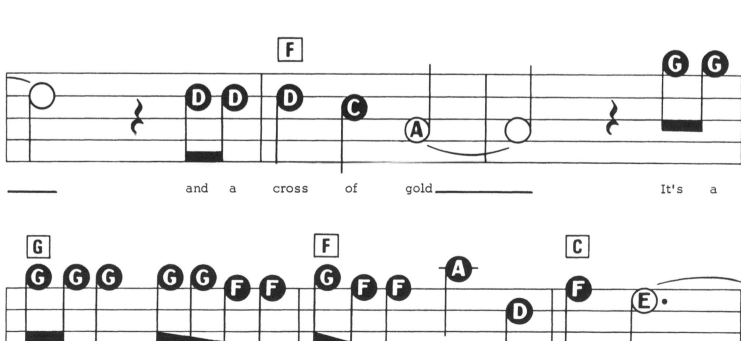

_____ and a cross of gold_____ It's a

pit - y they did - n't give you quite e - nough in - for - ma - tion_____

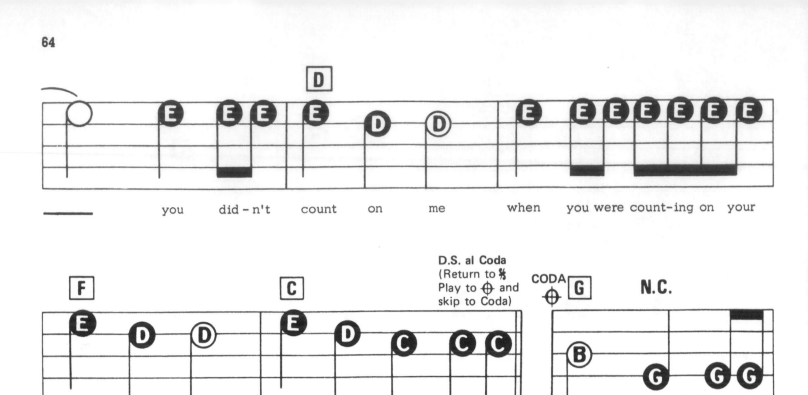

you did-n't count on me when you were count-ing on your

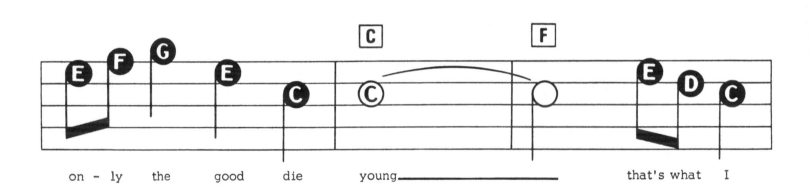

ro - sa - ry oh oh oh And they fun you know that

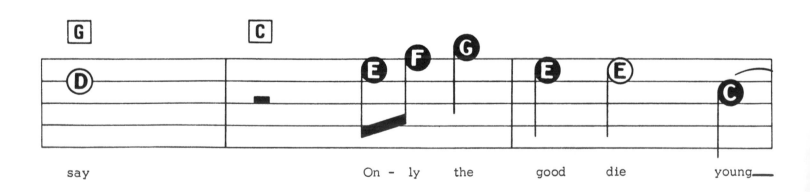

on - ly the good die young____ that's what I

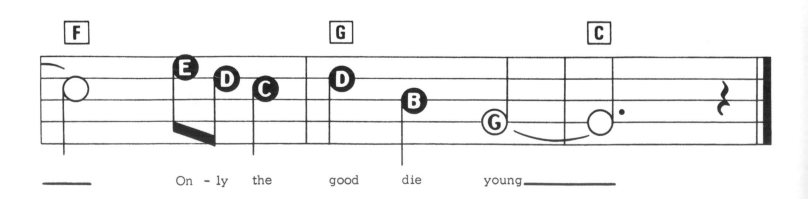

say On - ly the good die young__

___ On - ly the good die young____

Piano Man

Registration 4
Rhythm: Waltz

Words and Music by
Billy Joel

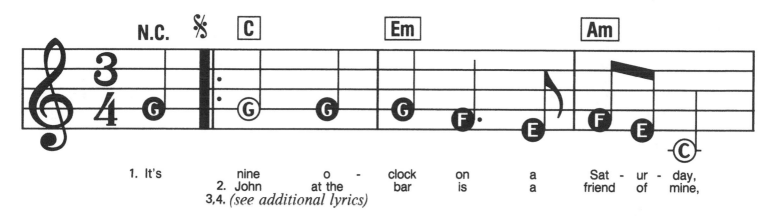

1. It's nine o - clock on a Sat - ur - day,
2. John at the bar is a friend of mine,
3,4. *(see additional lyrics)*

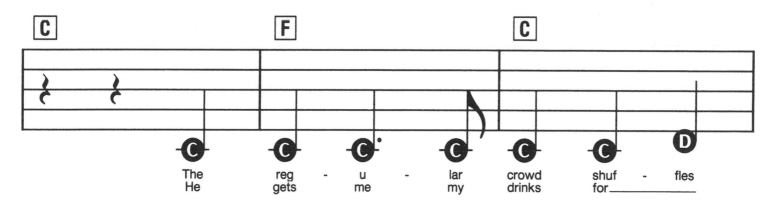

The reg - u - lar crowd shuf - fles
He gets me my drinks for_____

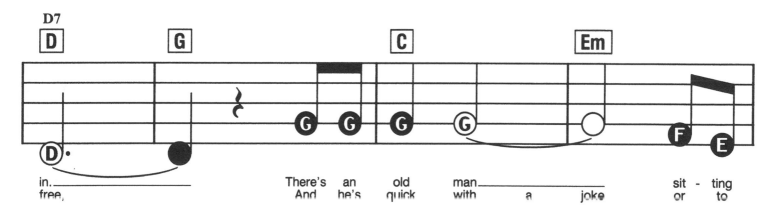

in._____ There's an old man_____ a joke sit - ting
free, And he's quick with a joke or to

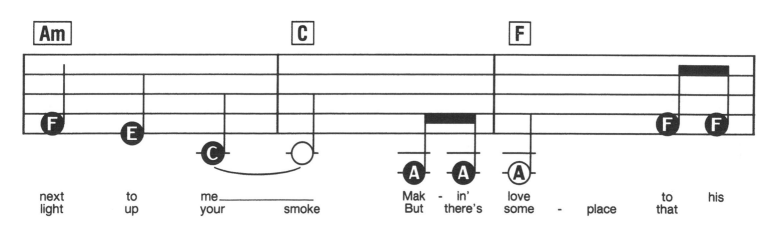

next to me_____ Mak - in' love to his
light up your smoke But there's some - place that

© 1973, 1974 JOEL SONGS
All Rights Controlled and Administered by EMI BLACKWOOD MUSIC INC.
All Rights Reserved   International Copyright Secured   Used by Permission

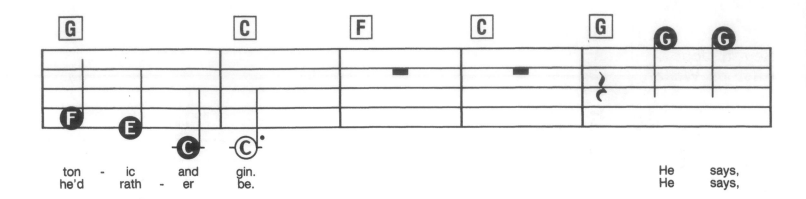

ton - ic and gin. He says,
he'd rath - er be. He says,

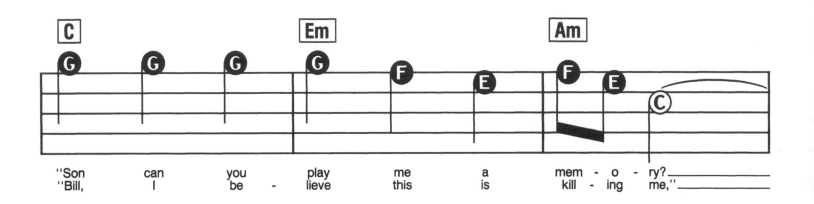

"Son can you play me a mem - o - ry?_____
"Bill, I be - lieve this is kill - ing me,"_____

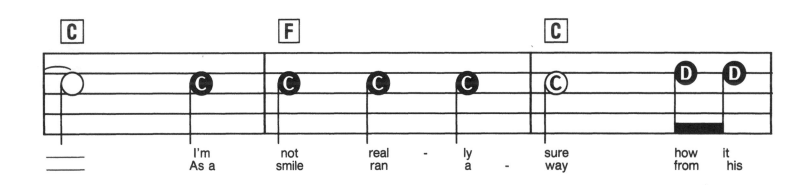

_____ I'm not real - ly sure how it
_____ As a smile ran a - way from his

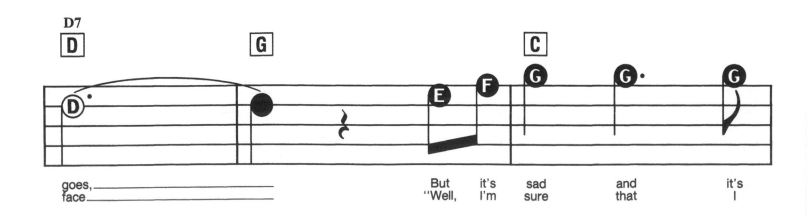

goes,_____ But it's sad and it's
face_____ "Well, I'm sure that I

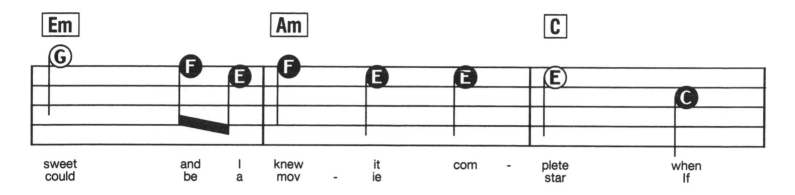

sweet / could and / be l / a knew / mov it / ie com / - plete / star when / If

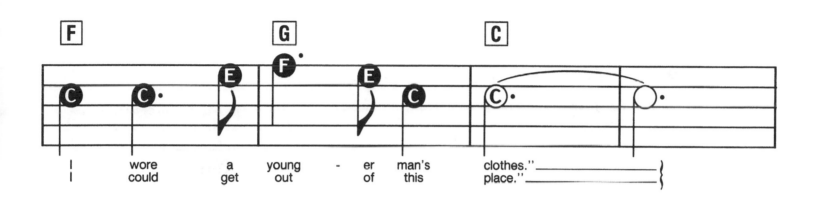

l / l wore / could a / get young / out - / of er / this man's / clothes." / place."

Chorus

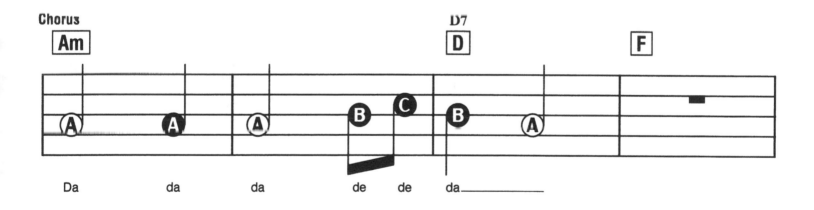

Da da da de de da

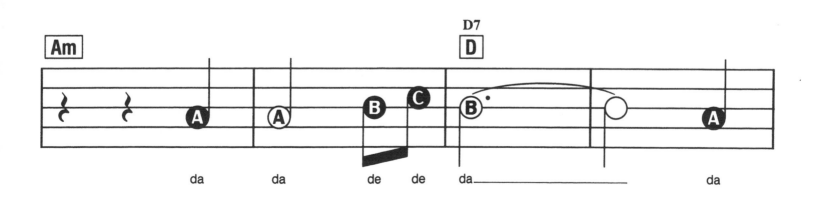

da da de de da da

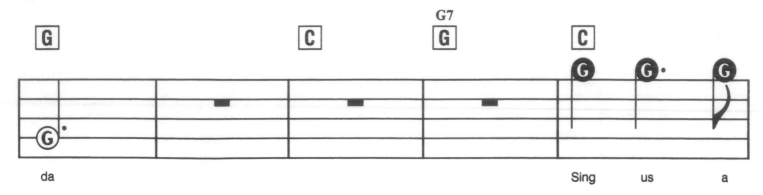

da   Sing   us   a

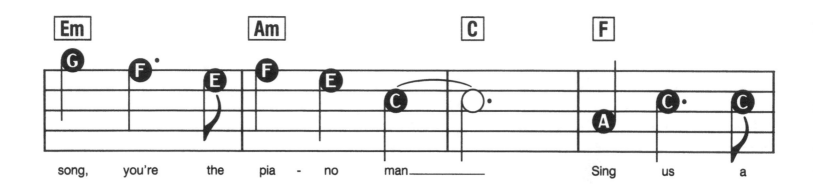

song,   you're   the   pia - no   man____   Sing   us   a

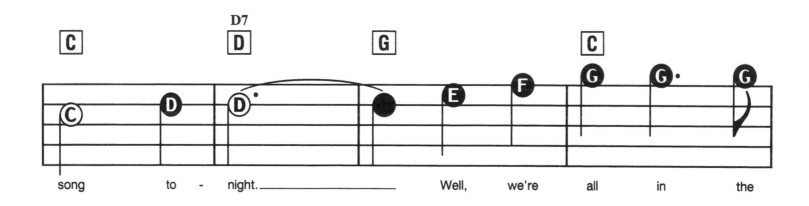

song   to - night.____   Well,   we're   all   in   the

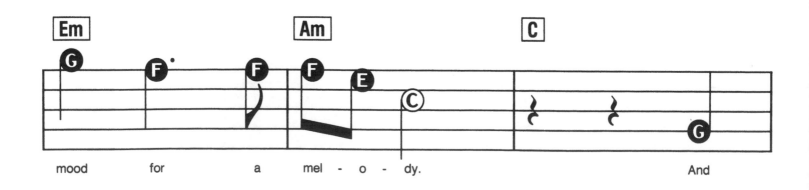

mood   for   a   mel - o - dy.   And

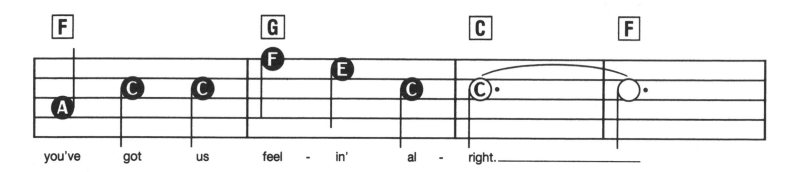

you've got us feel - in' al - right. _____

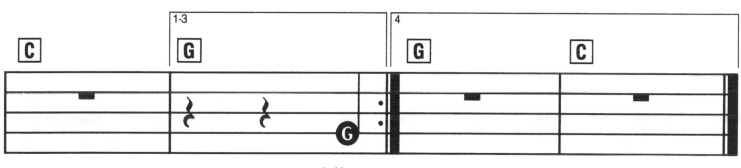

2. Now
3. Now

Additional Lyrics

3. Now Paul is a real estate novelist,
Who never had time for a wife,
And he's talkin' with Davey who's still in the Navy
And probably will be for life.
And the waitress is practicing politics,
As the businessmen slowly get stoned
Yes, they're sharing a drink they call loneliness
But it's better than drinkin' alone.

CHORUS

4. It's a pretty good crowd for a Saturday,
And the manager gives me a smile
'Cause he knows that it's me they've been comin' to see
To forget about life for a while.
And the piano sounds like a carnival
And the microphone smells like a beer
And they sit at the bar and put bread in my jar
And say "Man, what are you doin' here?"

CHORUS

Say Goodbye To Hollywood

Registration 8
Rhythm: Rock or 16 Beat

Words and Music by
Billy Joel

1. Bob - by's driv - in' through the cit - y to - night through the
2. John - ny's tak - in' care of things for a while and his
3. *(See additional lyrics)*

lights in a hot new rent - a - car.
style is so right for trou - ba - dours.

He joins the lov - ers in his heav - y ma - chine, it's a
They got him sit - ting with his back to the door and he

scene down on Sun - set Boul - e - vard.
won't be my fast gun an - y - more.

Say good - bye to Hol -

© 1976 JOEL SONGS
This arrangement Copyright © 1991 JOEL SONGS
All Rights Controlled and Administered by EMI BLACKWOOD MUSIC INC.
All Rights Reserved   International Copyright Secured   Used by Permission

71

ly - wood, Say good - bye my ba - by;

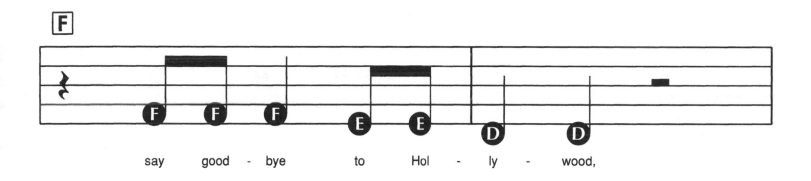

say good - bye to Hol - ly - wood,

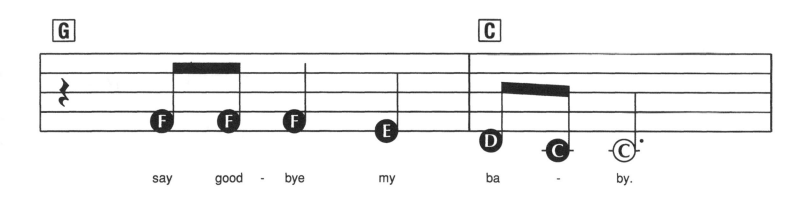

say good - bye my ba - by.

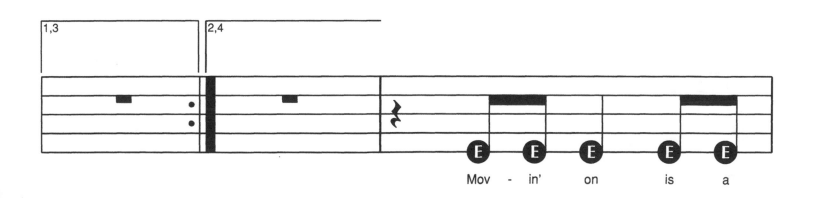

Mov - in' on is a

72

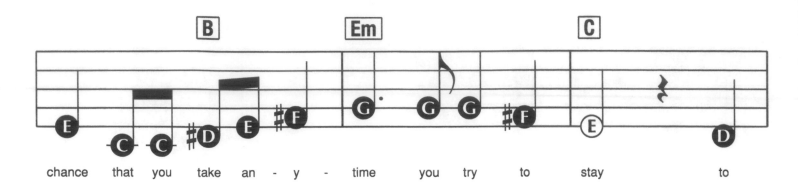

chance that you take an - y - time you try to stay to

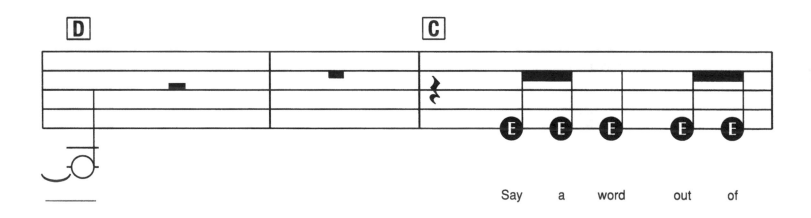

geth - er, whoa. _____

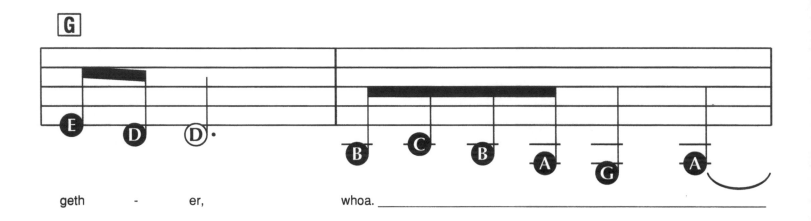

_____ Say a word out of

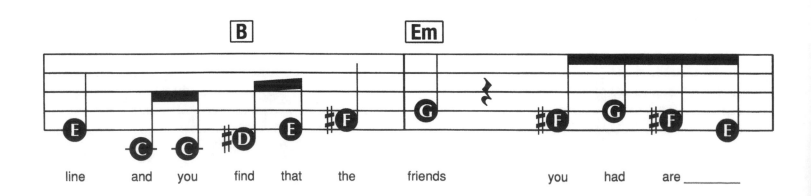

line and you find that the friends you had are _____

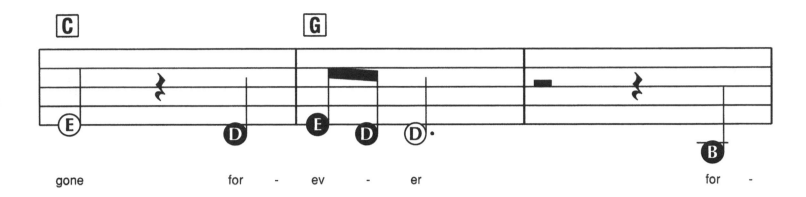

gone   for - ev - er   for -

D.C. (Repeat from beginning for 3rd verse and instrumental Last time D.C. and fade)

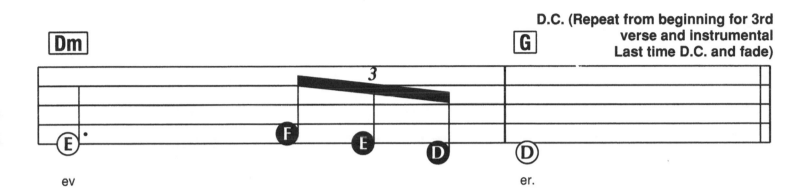

ev   er.

Additional Lyrics

3. So many faces in and out of my life
   Some will last some will just be now and then.
   Life is a series of hellos and goodbyes
   I'm afraid it's time for goodbye again.

4. Instrumental

She's Always A Woman

Registration 4
Rhythm: Waltz

Words and Music by
Billy Joel

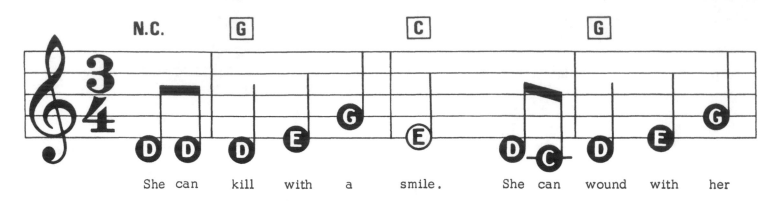

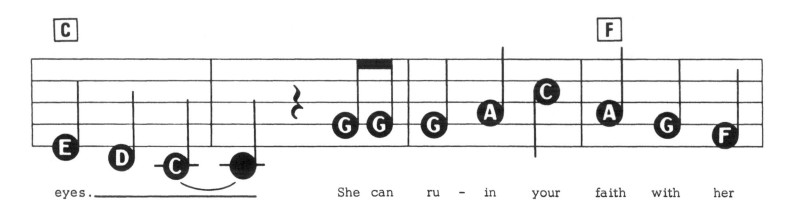

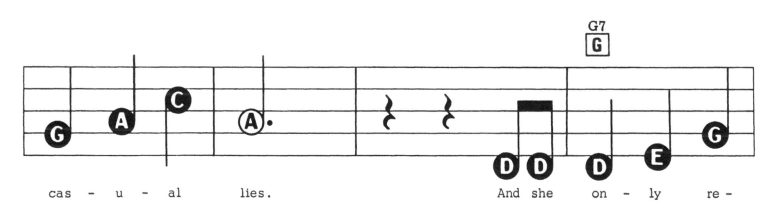

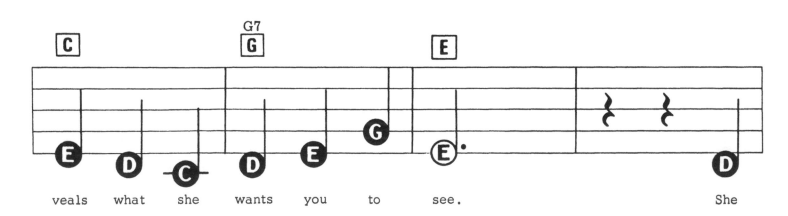

© 1977, 1978 IMPULSIVE MUSIC
All Rights Controlled and Administered by EMI APRIL MUSIC INC.
All Rights Reserved   International Copyright Secured   Used by Permission

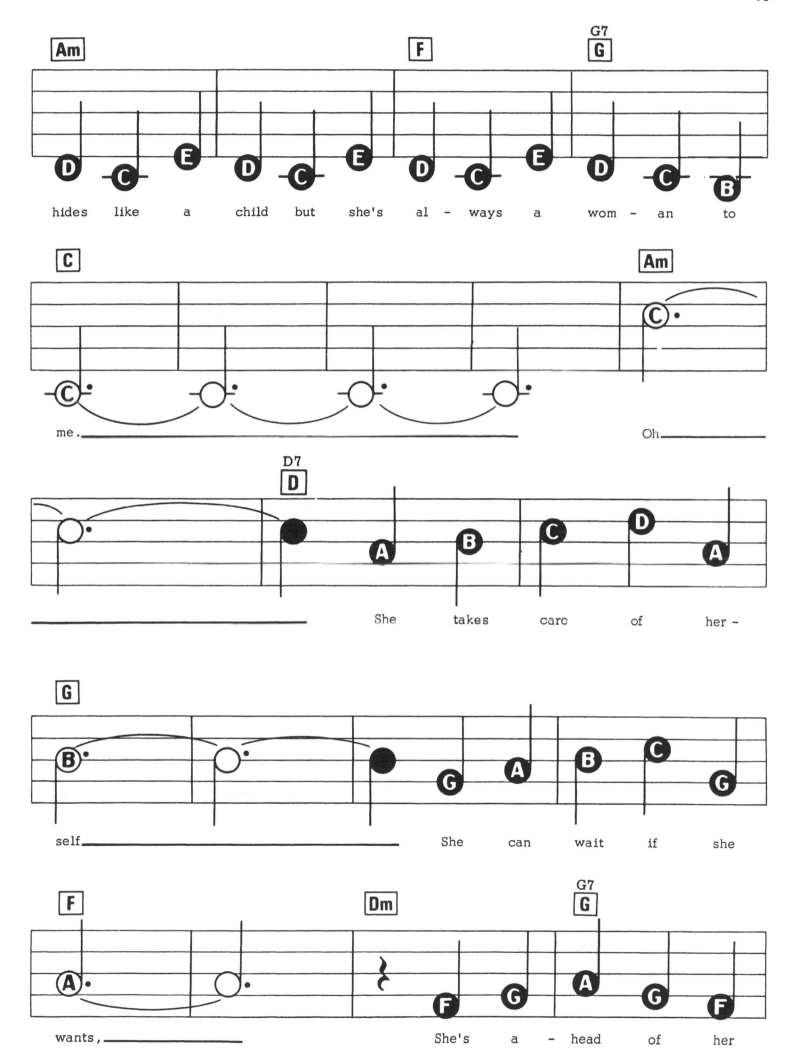

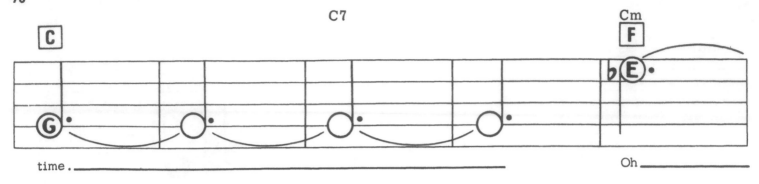

time. _____ Oh ____

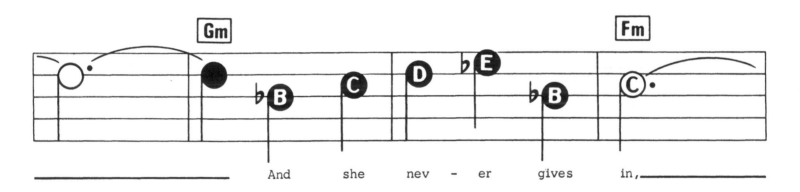

_____ And she nev – er gives out _____

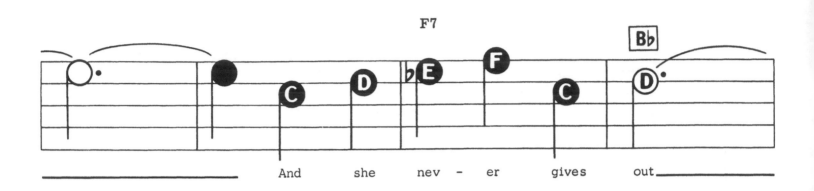

_____ And she nev – er gives in, _____

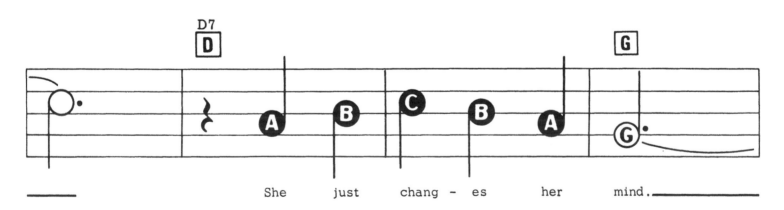

____ She just chang – es her mind. _____

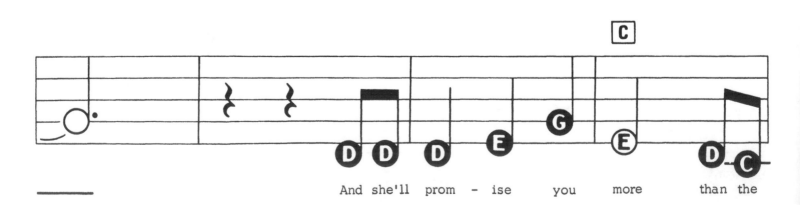

____ And she'll prom – ise you more than the

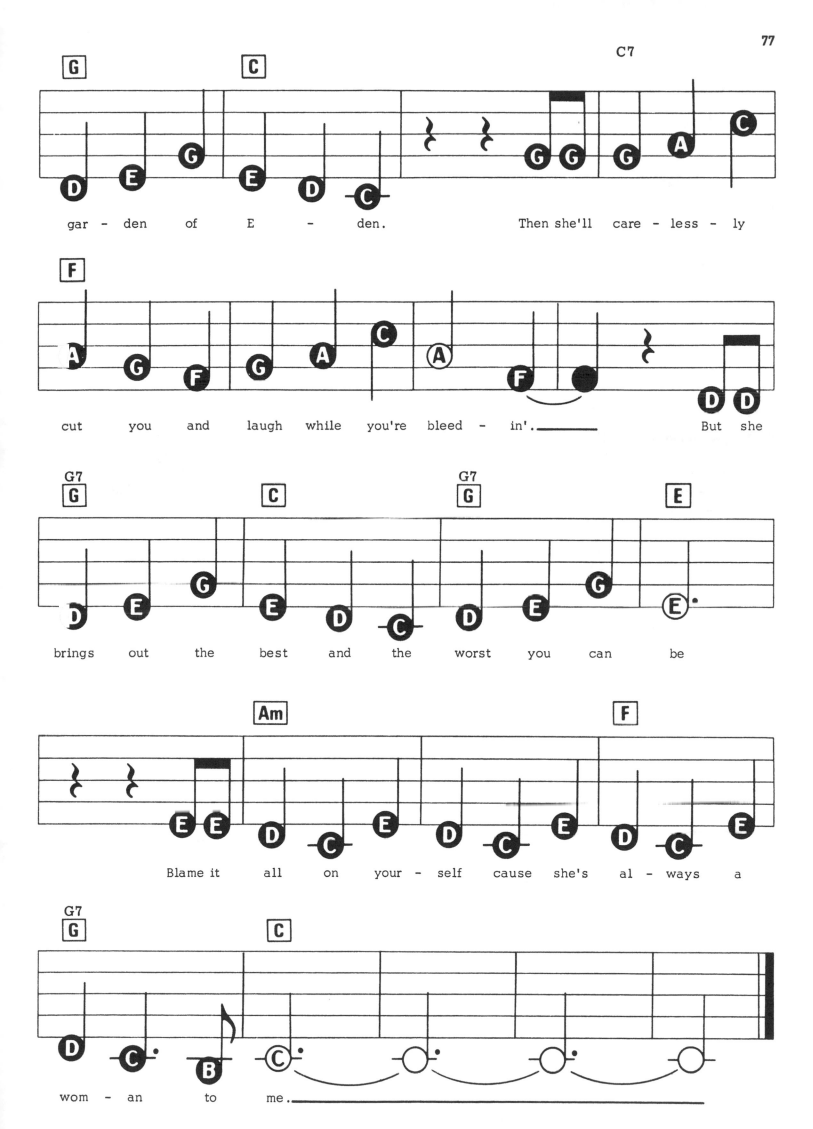

She's Got A Way

Registration 3
Rhythm: Rock or 8 Beat

Words and Music by
Billy Joel

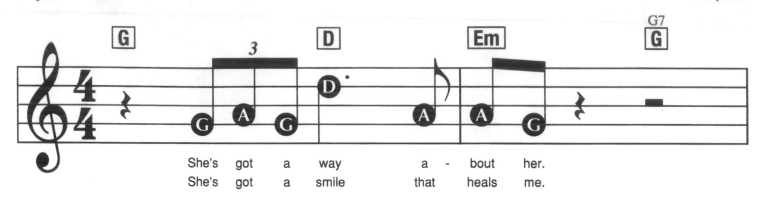

She's got a way a - bout her.
She's got a smile that heals me.

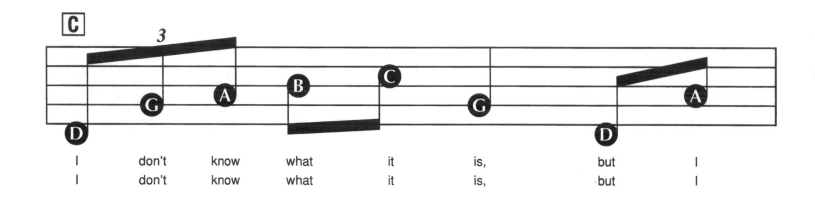

I don't know what it is, but I
I don't know what it is, but I

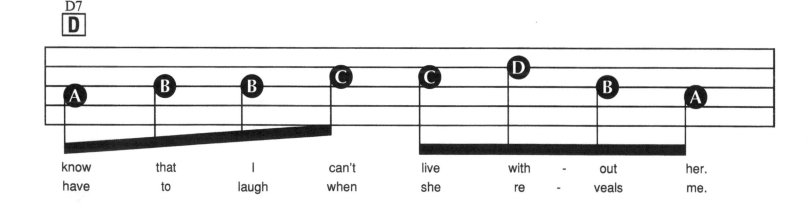

know that I can't live with - out her.
have to laugh when she re - veals me.

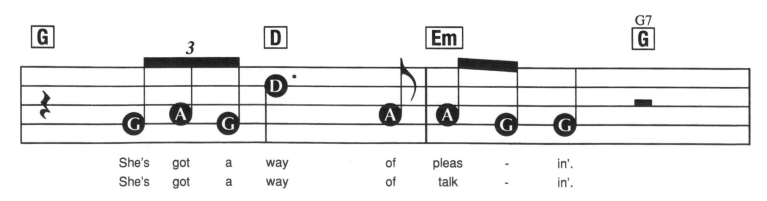

She's got a way of pleas - in'.
She's got a way of talk - in'.

© 1971, 1981 IMPULSIVE MUSIC
This arrangement Copyright © 1991 IMPULSIVE MUSIC
All Rights Administered and Controlled by EMI APRIL MUSIC INC.
All Rights Reserved   International Copyright Secured   Used by Permission
easy piano 1988 arr.

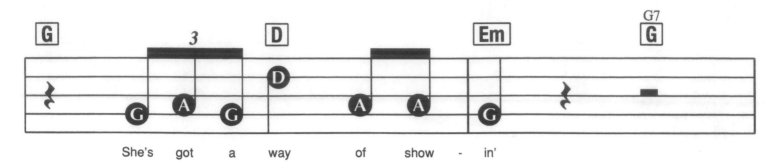

She's got a way of show - in'

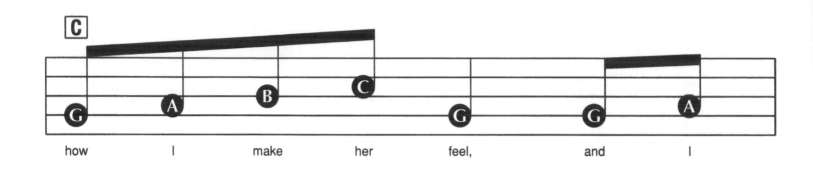

how I make her feel, and I

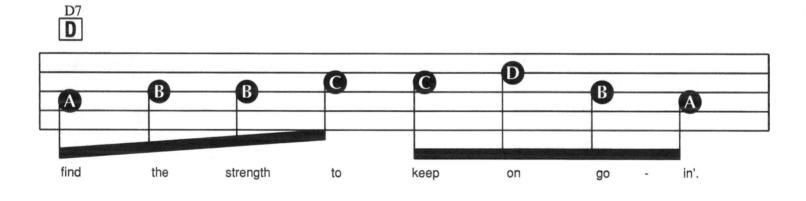

find the strength to keep on go - in'.

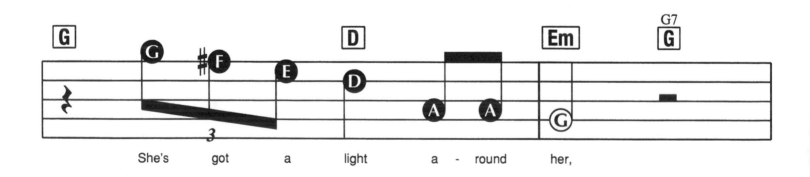

She's got a light a - round her,

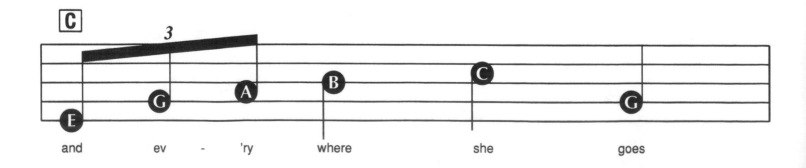

and ev - 'ry where she goes

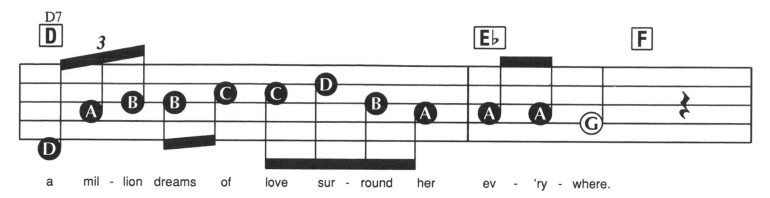

a mil - lion dreams of love sur - round her ev - 'ry - where.

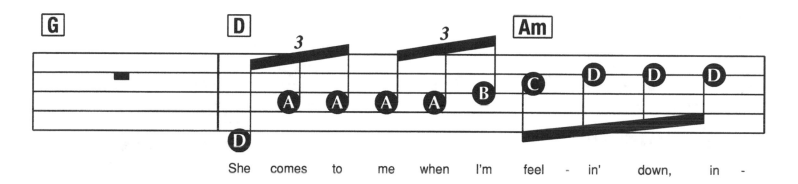

She comes to me when I'm feel - in' down, in -

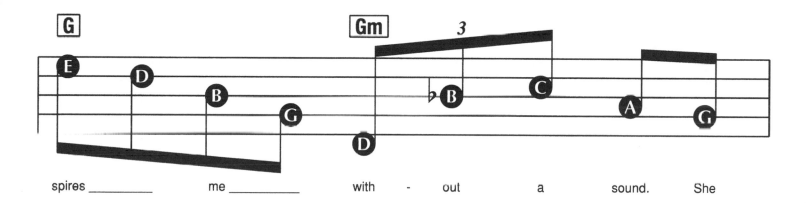

spires _____ me _____ with - out a sound. She

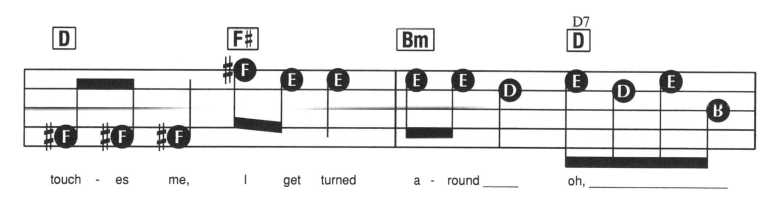

touch - es me, I get turned a - round _____ oh, _____

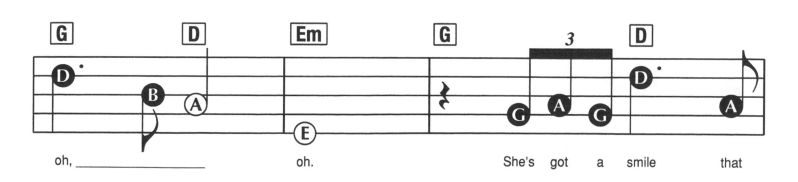

oh, _____ oh. She's got a smile that

heals me. I don't know why it is, but I

have to laugh when she re - veals me.

She's got a way a - bout her.

I don't know what it is, but I

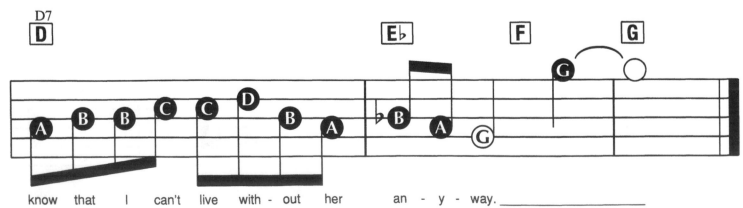

know that I can't live with - out her an - y - way. _____

Tell Her About It

Registration 4
Rhythm: Fox Trot or Swing

Words and Music by
Billy Joel

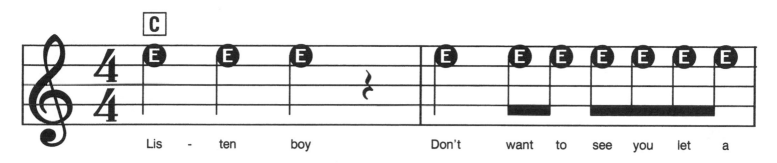

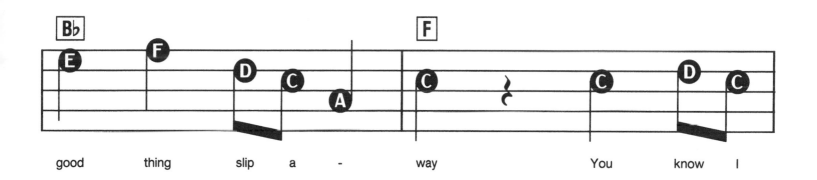

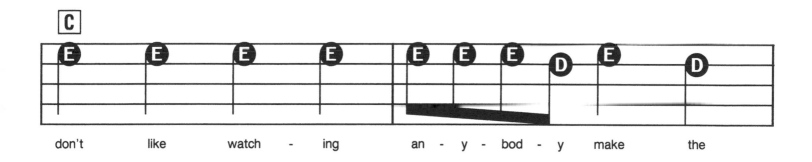

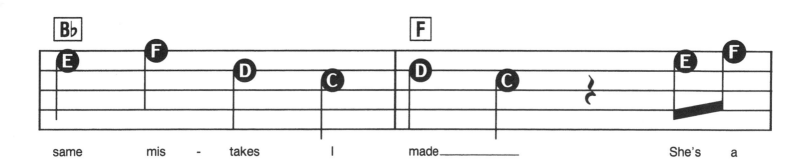

© 1983 JOEL SONGS
All Rights Controlled and Administered by EMI BLACKWOOD MUSIC INC.
All Rights Reserved   International Copyright Secured   Used by Permission

84

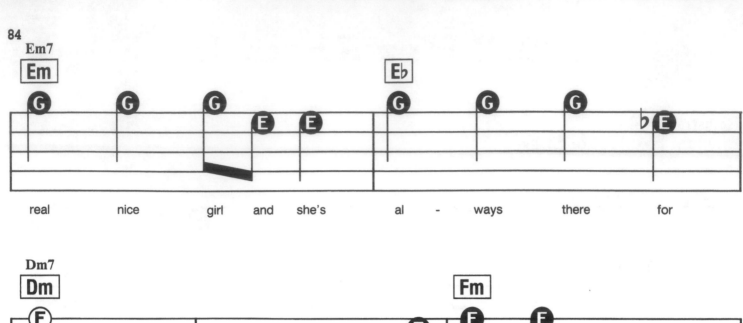

real   nice   girl   and she's   al - ways   there   for

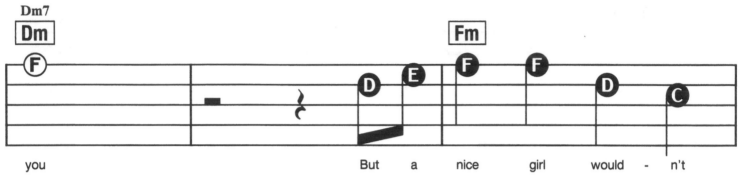

you   But   a   nice   girl would - n't

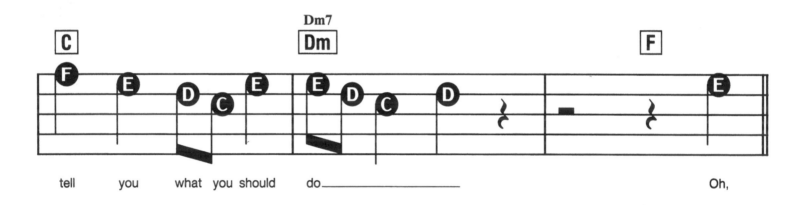

tell   you   what you should   do_____   Oh,

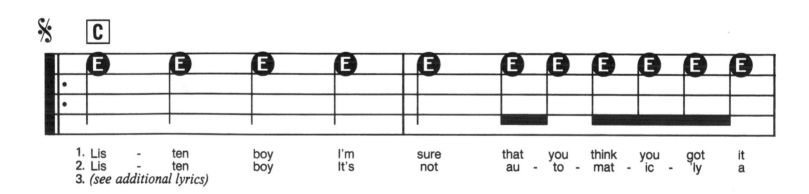

1. Lis - ten   boy   I'm   sure   that you think you got   it
2. Lis - ten   boy   It's   not   au - to - mat - ic - 'ly a
3. *(see additional lyrics)*

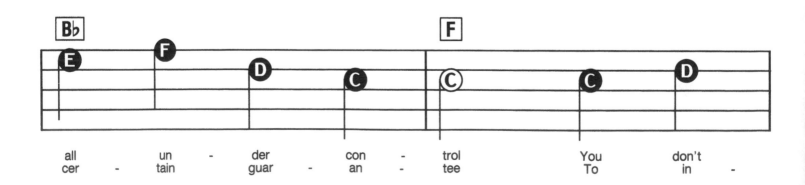

all   un - der   con - trol   You   don't
cer - tain   guar - an - tee   To   in -

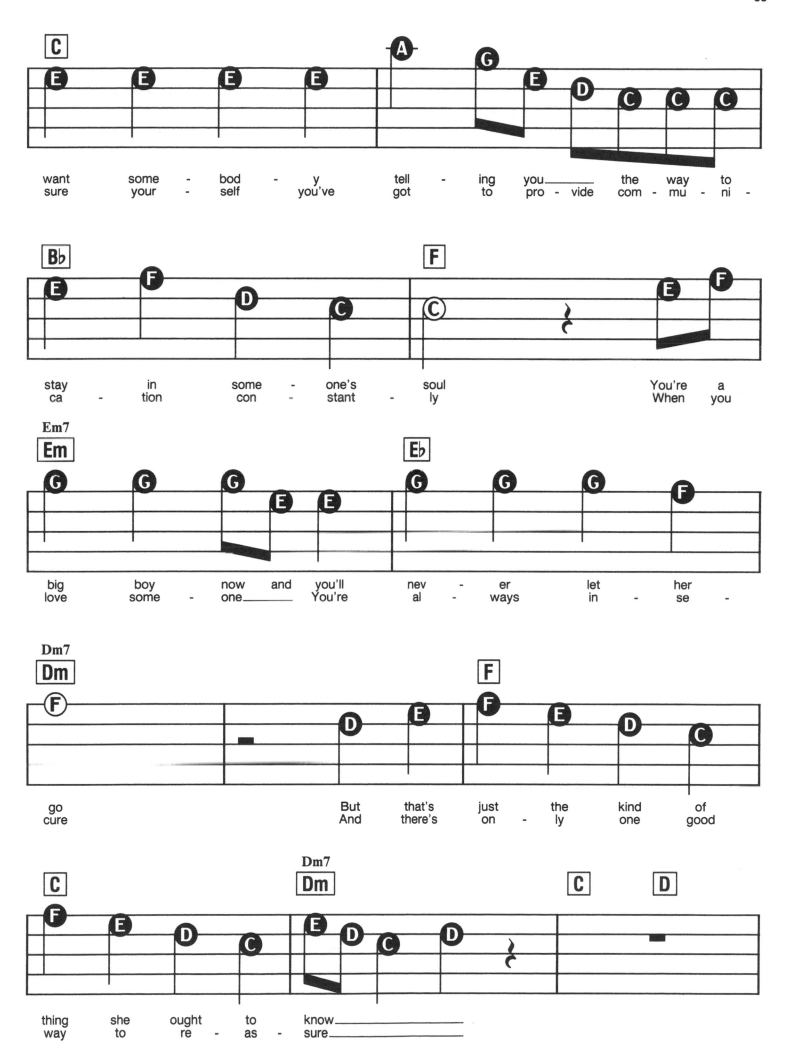

Chorus

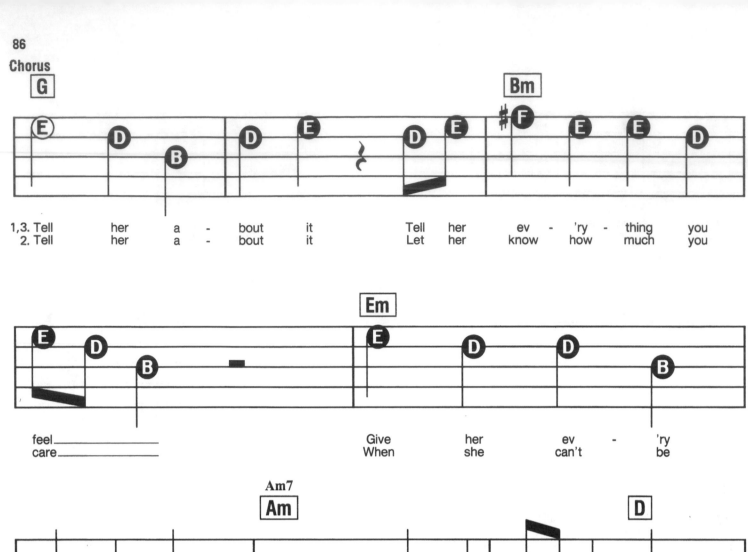

1,3. Tell her a - bout it　　Tell her ev - 'ry - thing you
2. Tell her a - bout it　　Let her know how much you

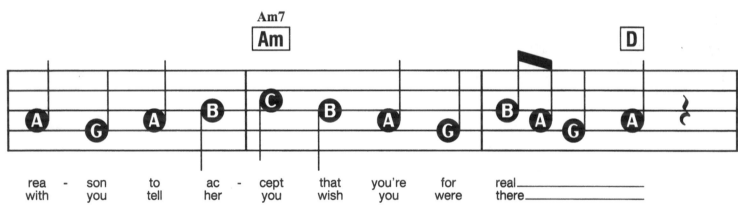

feel＿＿＿　　　　Give her ev - 'ry
care＿＿＿　　　　When she can't be

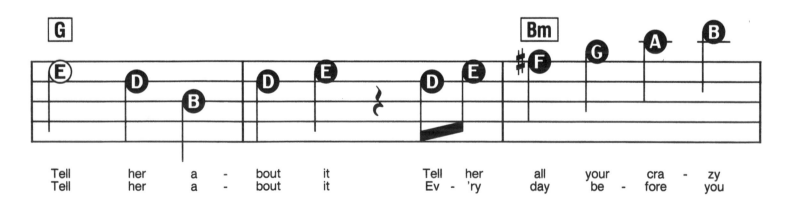

rea - son to ac - cept that you're for real＿＿＿
with you tell her you wish you were there＿＿＿

Tell her a - bout it　　Tell her all your cra - zy
Tell her a - bout it　　Ev - 'ry day be - fore you

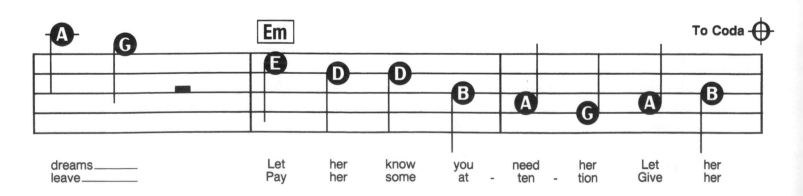

To Coda ⊕

dreams＿＿　　Let her know you need her Let her
leave＿＿　　Pay her some at - ten - tion Give her

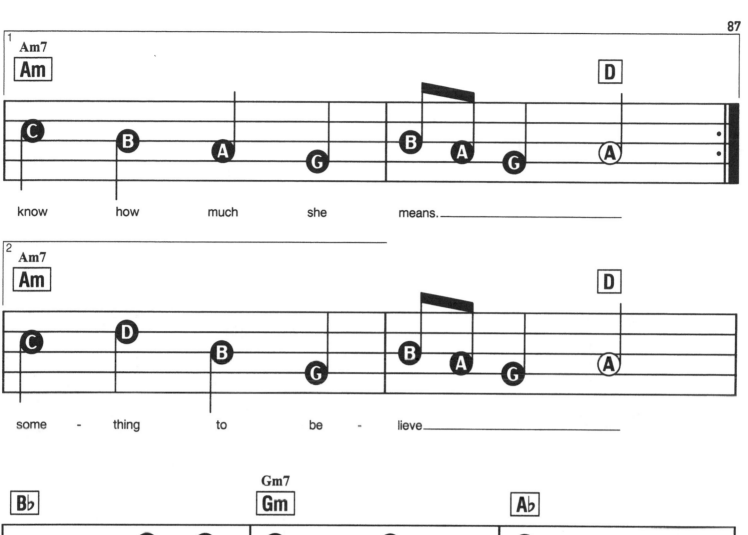

know how much she means._____

some - thing to be - lieve_____

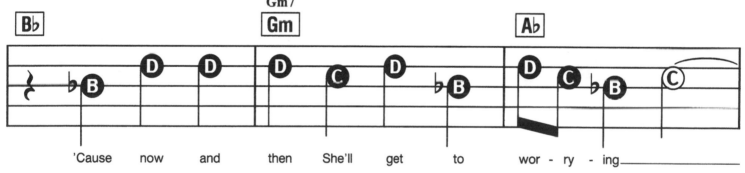

'Cause now and then She'll get to wor - ry - ing_____

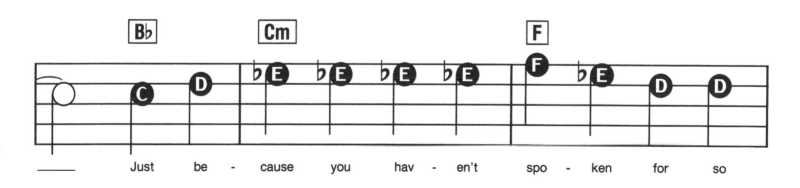

_____ Just be - cause you hav - en't spo - ken for so

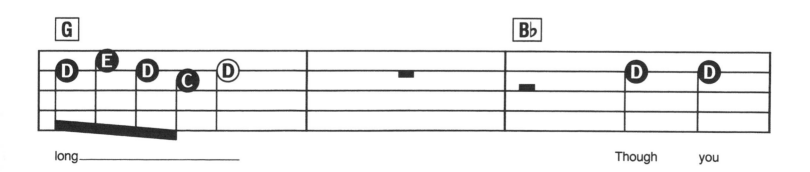

long_____ Though you

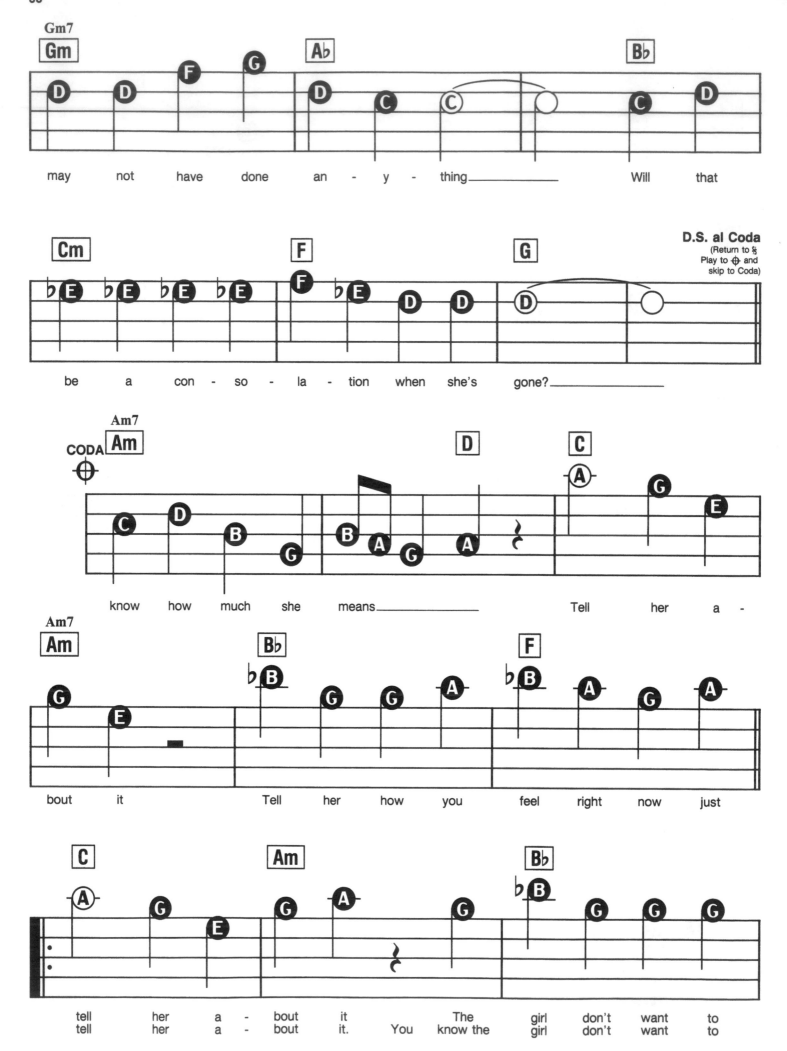

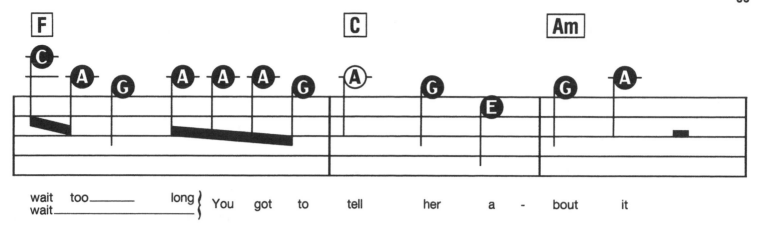

wait too_____ long
wait_____ You got to tell her a - bout it

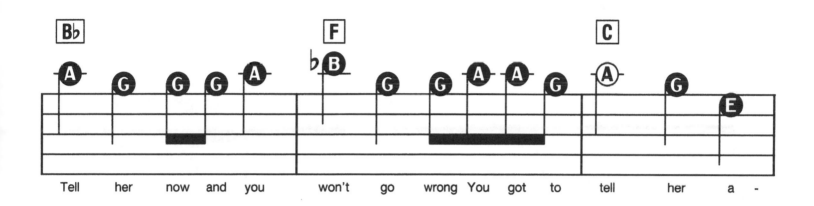

Tell her now and you won't go wrong You got to tell her a -

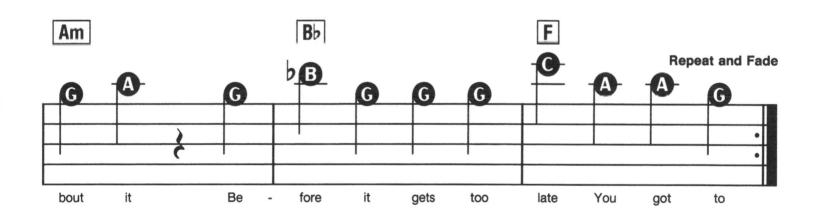

bout it Be - fore it gets too late You got to

Additional Lyrics

Listen boy it's good information from a
Man who's made mistakes
Just a word or two that she get from you
Could be the difference that it makes
She's a trusting soul she's put her trust in you
But a girl like that won't tell you what you should do.

CHORUS

We Didn't Start The Fire

Registration 5
Rhythm: Rock

Words and Music by
Billy Joel

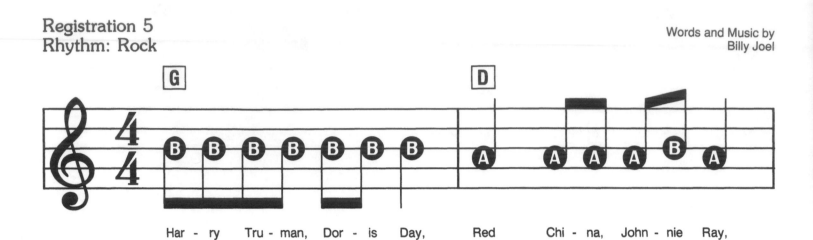

Har - ry Tru - man, Dor - is Day, Red Chi - na, John - nie Ray,

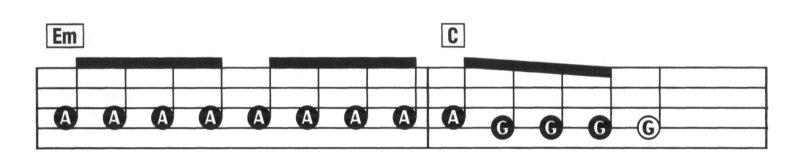

South Pa - cif - ic, Wal - ter Win - chell, Joe Di - Mag - gi - o.

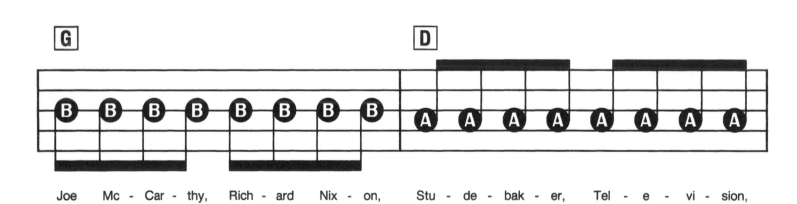

Joe Mc - Car - thy, Rich - ard Nix - on, Stu - de - bak - er, Tel - e - vi - sion,

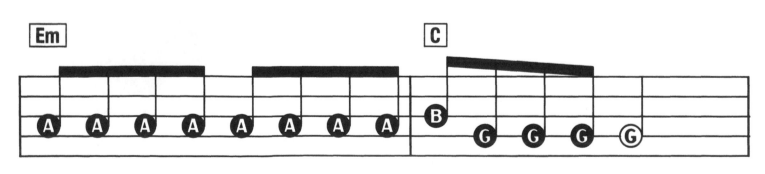

North Ko - re - a, South Ko - re - a, Mar - i - lyn Mon - roe.

© 1989 JOEL SONGS
All Rights Controlled and Administered by EMI BLACKWOOD MUSIC INC.
All Rights Reserved   International Copyright Secured   Used by Permission

Instrumental

Ro - sen - bergs,   H -   Bomb,
Bud - dy Holly,   Ben   Hur,

Sug - ar Ray,   Pan - mun - jom,   Bran - do, The King And   I,
Space   Monkey,   Ma - fi - a,   Hula - Hoops,   Cas - tro,

and The Catch - er In The Rye.   Ei - sen - how - er,   Vac - cine,
Ed - sel is a no go.   U - 2,   Syng - man Rhee,

Eng - land's got a new queen,   Mar - ci - an - o, Li - ber - a - ce,
pay - o - la and Ken - ne - dy.   Chub - by Check - er, Psy - cho,

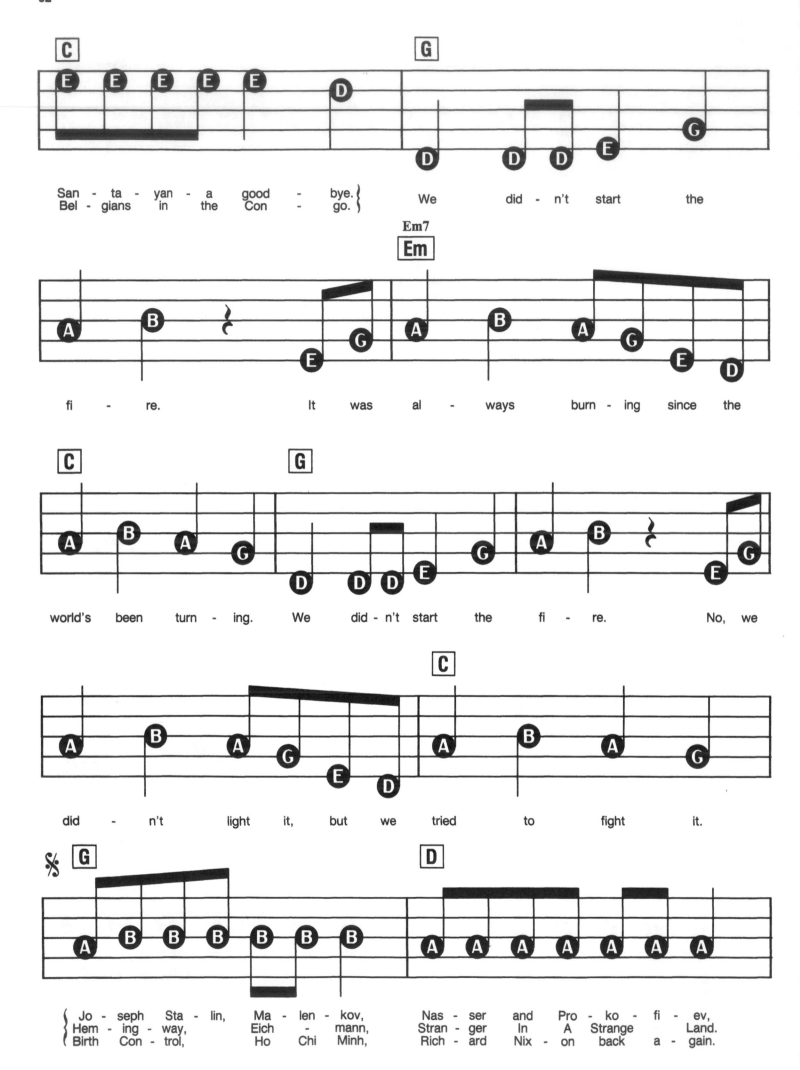

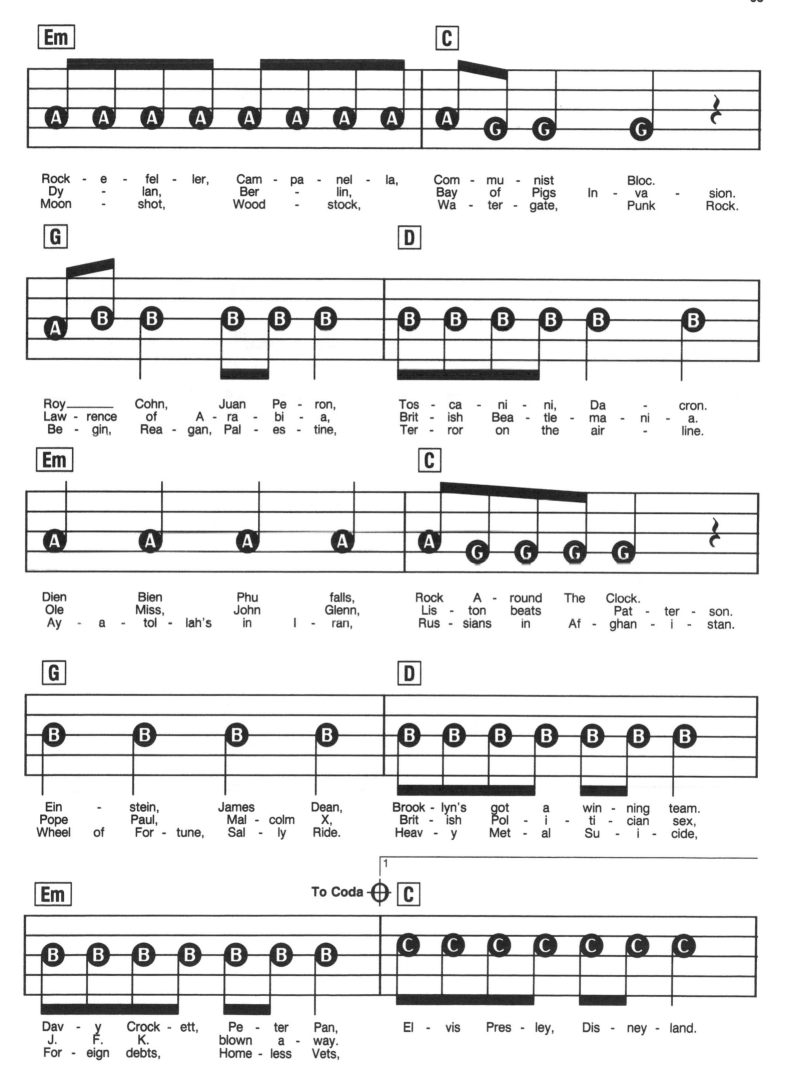

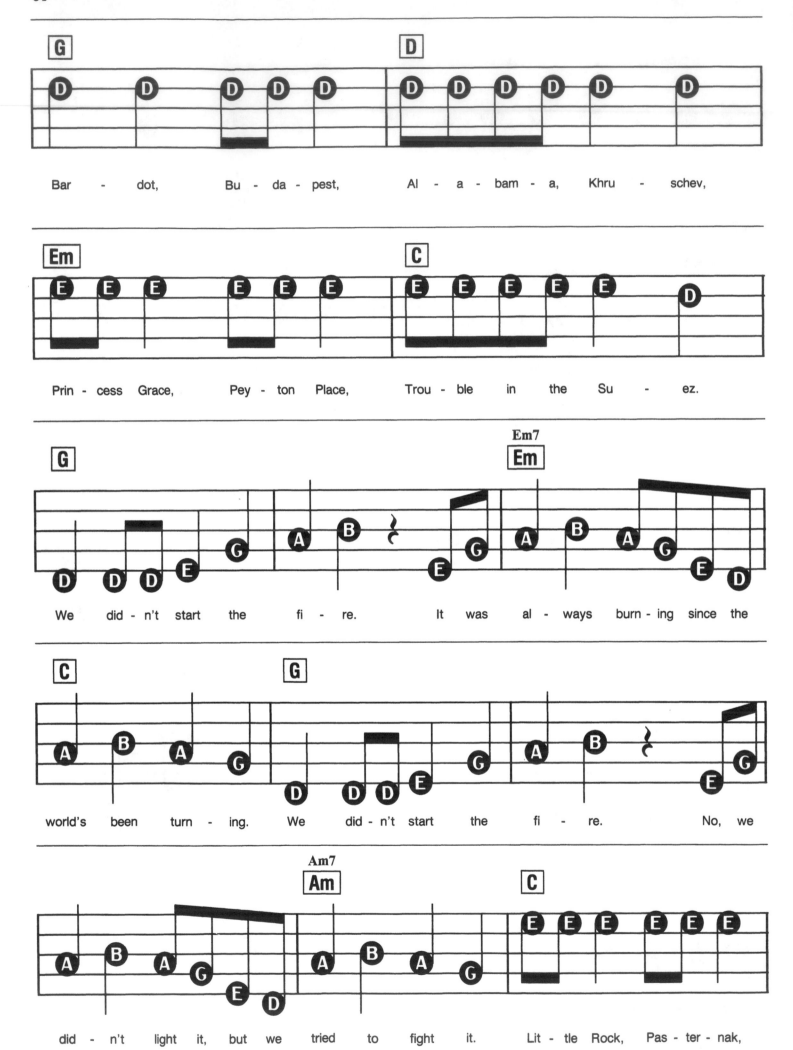

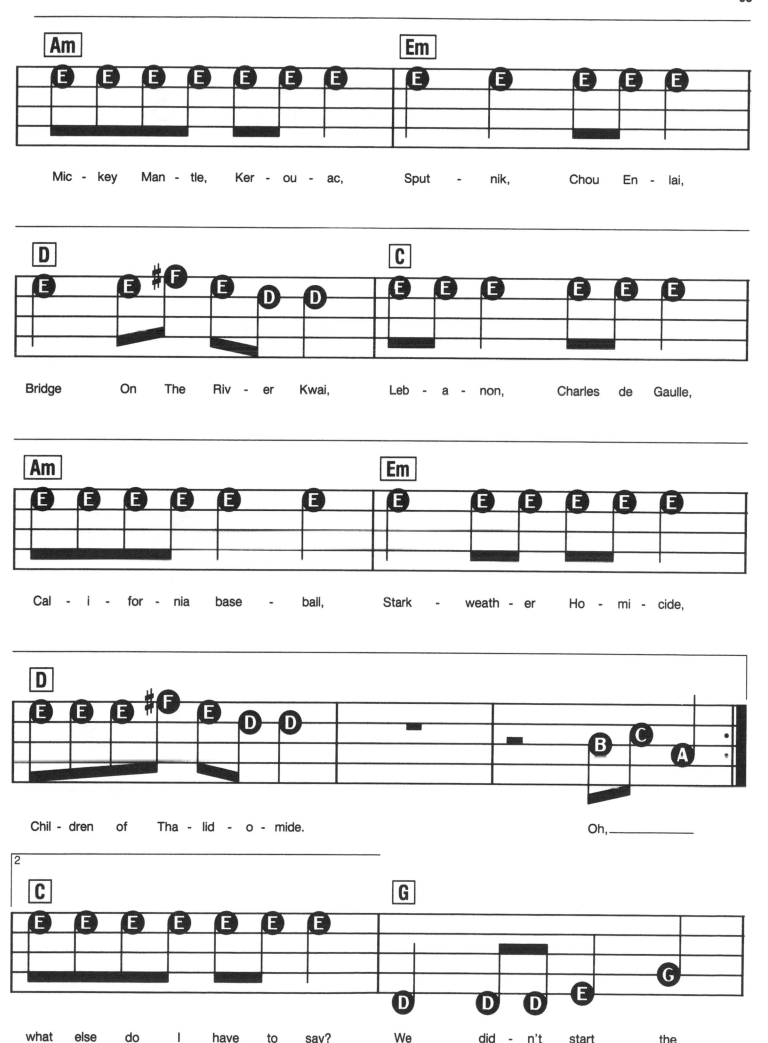

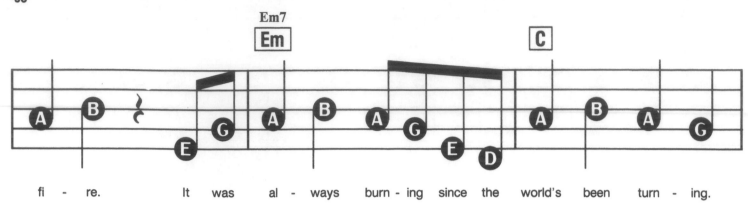

fi - re. It was al - ways burn - ing since the world's been turn - ing.

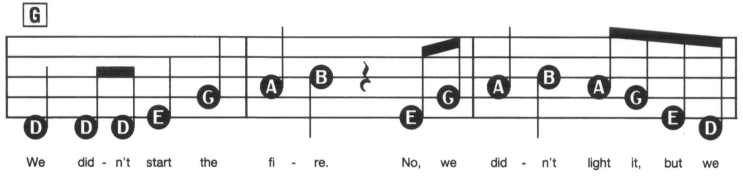

We did - n't start the fi - re. No, we did - n't light it, but we

D.S. al Coda
(Return to %
Play to ⊕ and
skip to Coda)

CODA
⊕

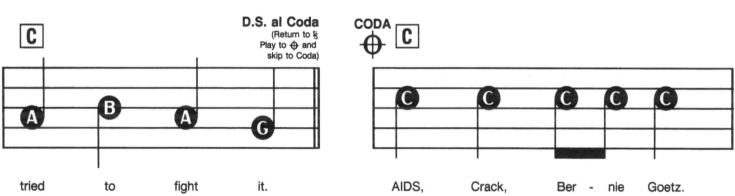

tried to fight it. AIDS, Crack, Ber - nie Goetz.

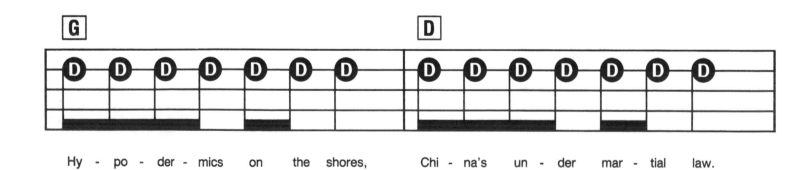

Hy - po - der - mics on the shores, Chi - na's un - der mar - tial law.

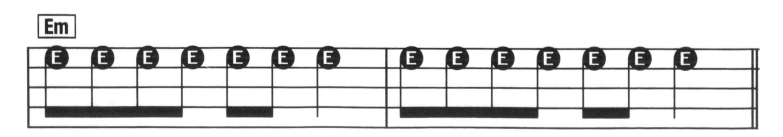

Rock and Roll - er Co - la Wars, I can't take it an - y - more.

You May Be Right

Registration 1
Rhythm: Rock or 8 Beat

Words and Music by
Billy Joel

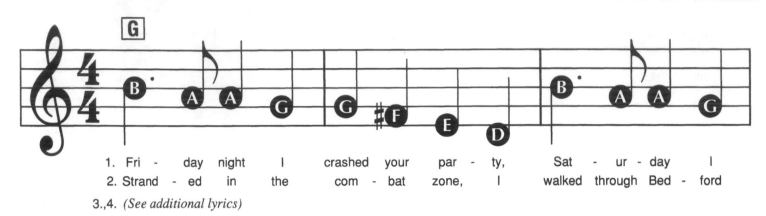

1. Fri - day night I crashed your par - ty, Sat - ur - day I
2. Strand - ed in the com - bat zone, I walked through Bed - ford

3.,4. *(See additional lyrics)*

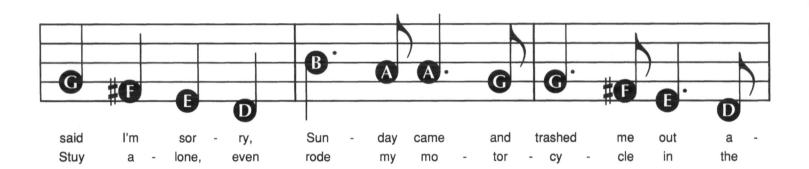

said I'm sor - ry, Sun - day came and trashed me out a -
Stuy a - lone, even rode my mo - tor - cy - cle in the

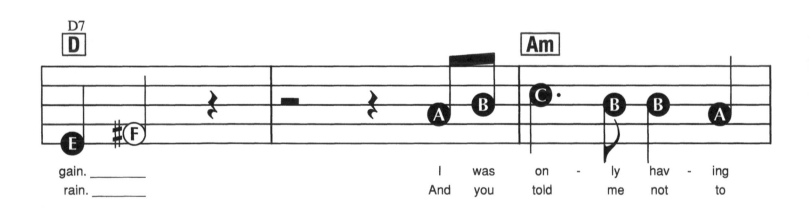

gain. _____ I was on - ly hav - ing
rain. _____ And you told me not to

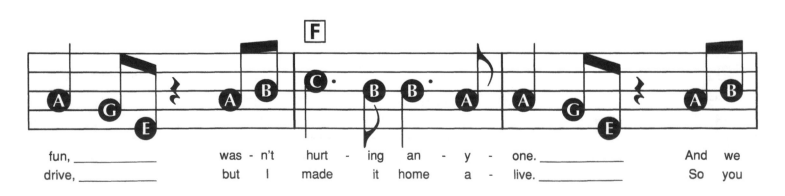

fun, _____ was - n't hurt - ing an - y - one. _____ And we
drive, _____ but I made it home a - live. _____ So you

© 1980 IMPULSIVE MUSIC
This arrangement Copyright © 1991 IMPULSIVE MUSIC
All Rights Administered and Controlled by EMI APRIL MUSIC INC.
All Rights Reserved   International Copyright Secured   Used by Permission

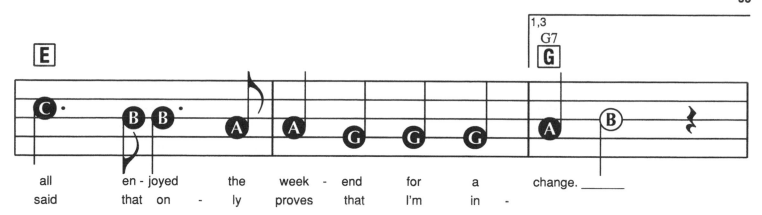

all en - joyed the week - end for a change. _____
said that on - ly proves that I'm in -

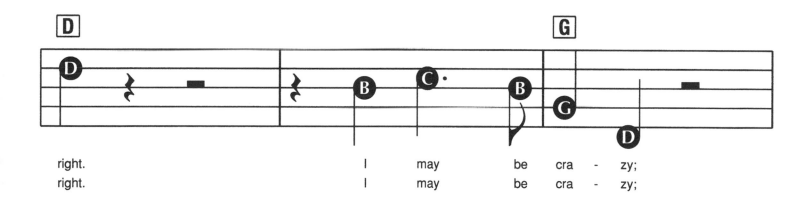

2. I've been sane. _____
2.,5. You may be
4. You may be

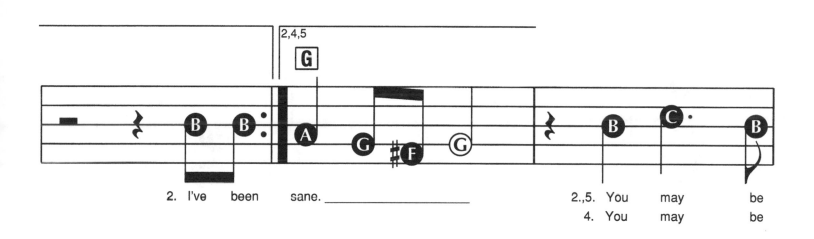

right.
right.
I may be cra - zy;
I may be cra - zy;

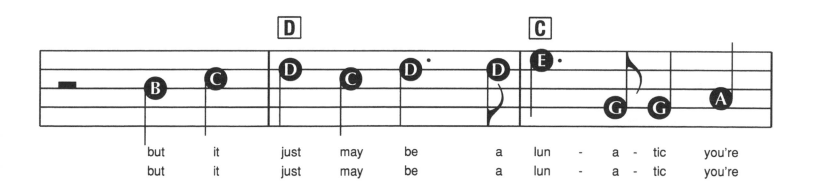

but it just may be a lun - a - tic you're
but it just may be a lun - a - tic you're

100

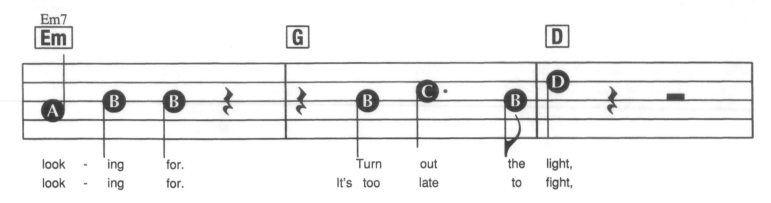

look - ing for.
look - ing for.
Turn out the light,
It's too late to fight,

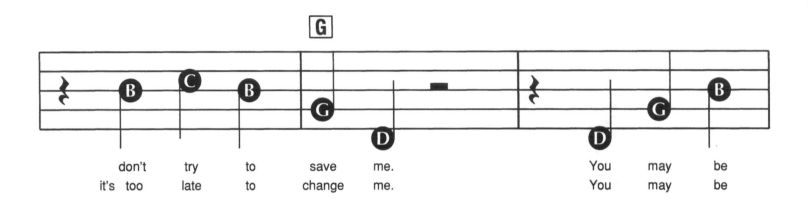

don't try to save me.
it's too late to change me.
You may be
You may be

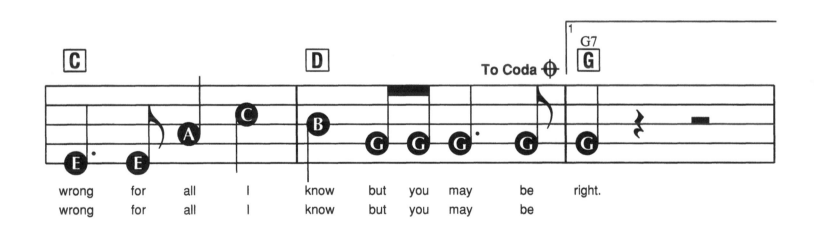

To Coda ⊕

wrong for all I know but you may be right.
wrong for all I know but you may be

D.C.
(Return to the beginning)

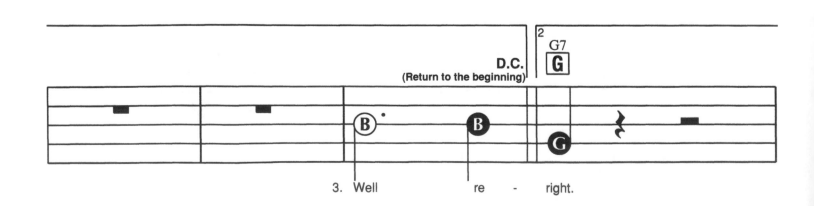

3. Well re - right.

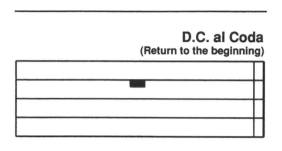

D.C. al Coda
(Return to the beginning)

CODA

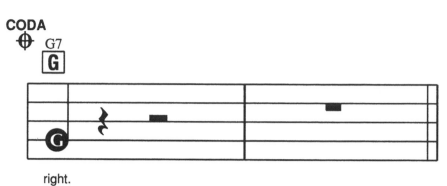

right.

Repeat and Fade

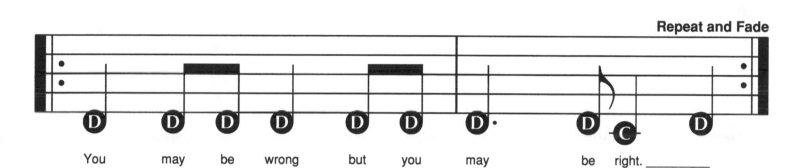

You   may   be   wrong   but   you   may   be   right. _____

Additional Lyrics

3. Remember how I found you there;
    Alone in your electric chair.
    I told you dirty jokes until you smiled.
    You were lonely for a man,
    I said, "take me as I am."
    'Cause you might enjoy some madness for a while.

4. Now think of all the years you tried
    To find someone to satisfy you.
    I might be as crazy as you say.
    If I'm crazy then it's true,
    That's all because of you.
    And you wouldn't want me any other way.

5. *Instrumental*

You're Only Human

Registration 4
Rhythm: Shuffle or 12 Beat

Words and Music by
Billy Joel

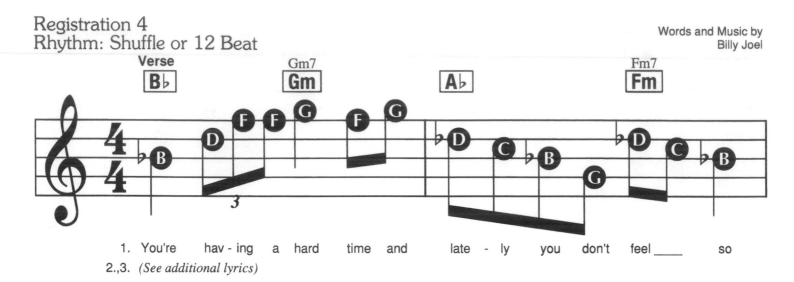

1. You're hav-ing a hard time and late-ly you don't feel ____ so

2.,3. *(See additional lyrics)*

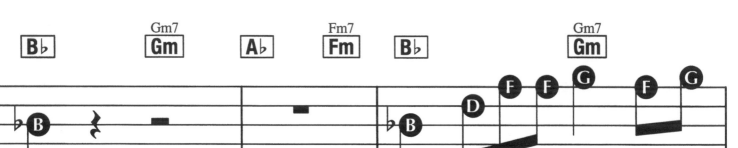

good.   You're get-ting a bad rep-u-

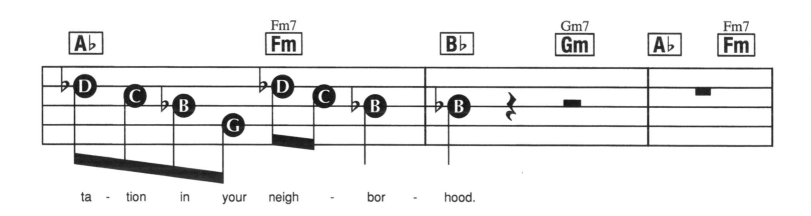

ta-tion in your neigh-bor-hood.

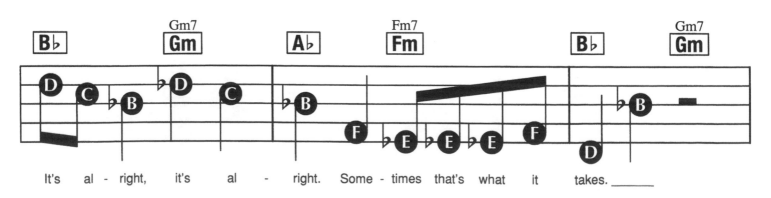

It's al-right, it's al-right. Some-times that's what it takes. _____

© 1985 by JOEL SONGS
This arrangement Copyright © 1991 JOEL SONGS
All Rights Controlled and Administered by EMI BLACKWOOD MUSIC INC.
All Rights Reserved   International Copyright Secured   Used by Permission

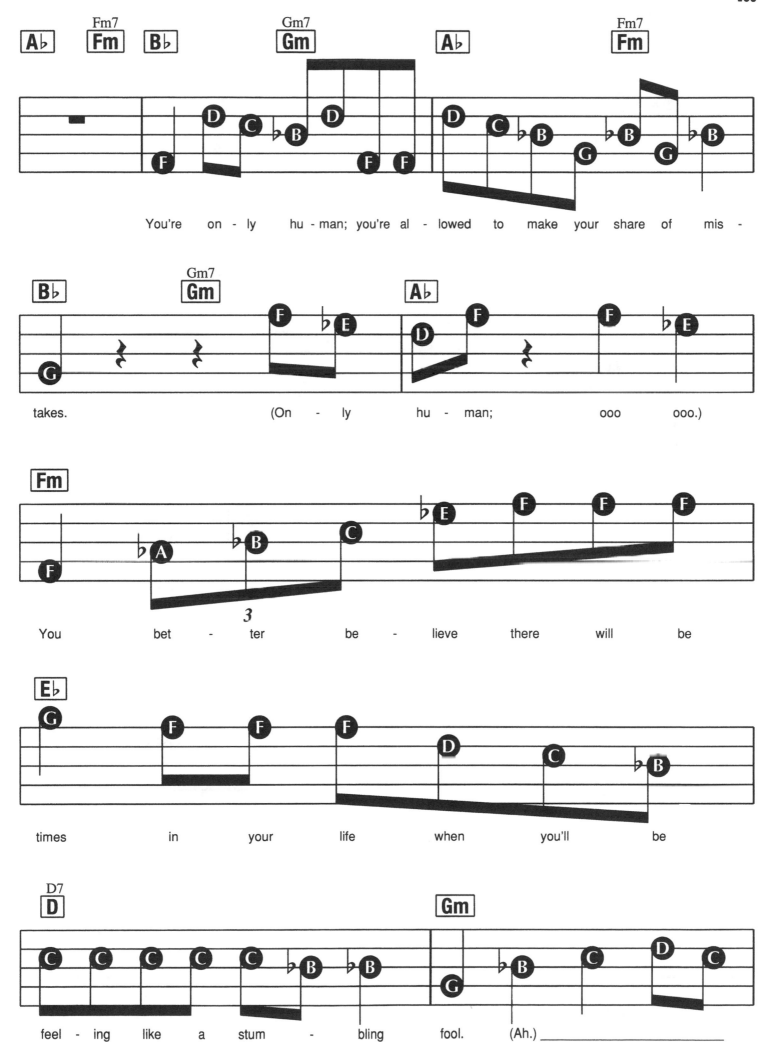

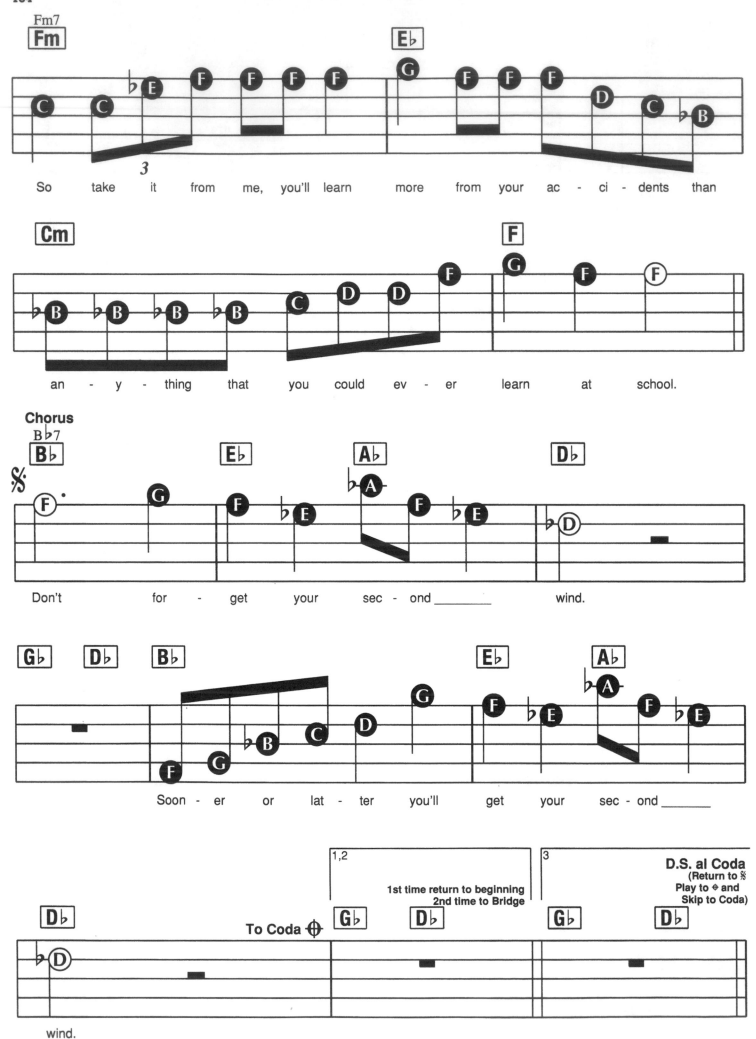

Bridge

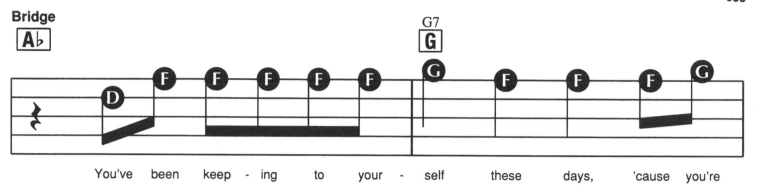

You've been keep - ing to your - self these days, 'cause you're

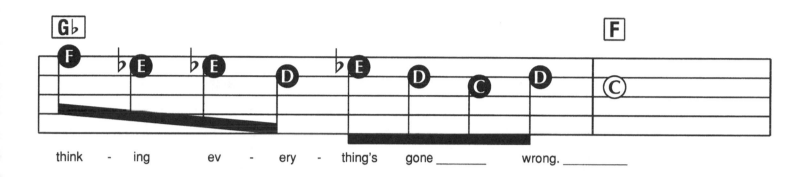

think - ing ev - ery - thing's gone _____ wrong. _____

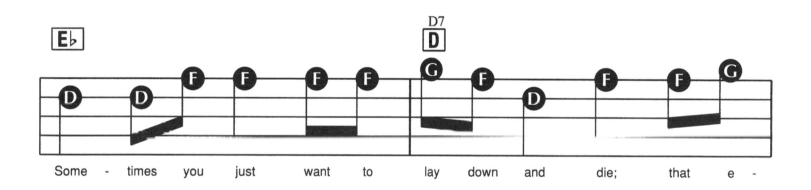

Some - times you just want to lay down and die; that e -

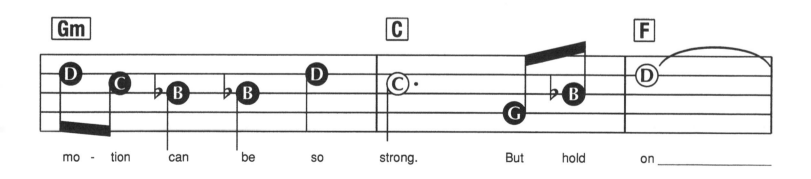

mo - tion can be so strong. But hold on _____

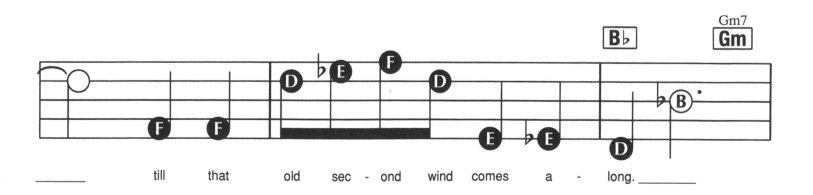

_____ till that old sec - ond wind comes a - long. _____

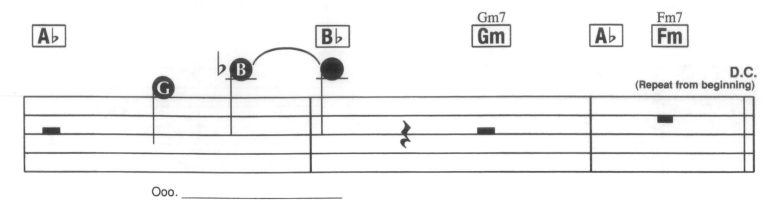

Ooo. _____

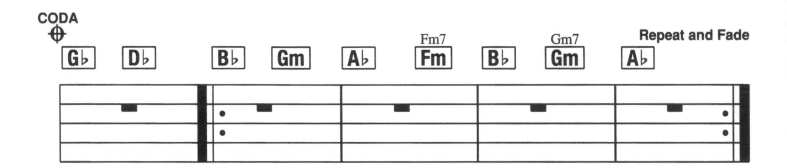

Additional Lyrics

Verse 2:

It's not always easy to be living in this
World of pain.
You're gonna be crashing into stone walls
Again and again.
It's alright, it's alright,
Though you feel your heart break.
You're only human, you're gonna have to
Deal with heartache.
Just like a boxer in a title fight;
You got to walk in that ring all alone
You're not the only one who's made
Mistakes.
But they're the only things that you can
Truly call your own.

Verse 3:

You probably don't want to hear advice
From someone else.
But I wouldn't be telling you if I hadn't
Been there myself.
It's alright it's alright;
Sometimes that's all it takes.
We're only human,
We're supposed to make mistakes.
But I survived all those long lonely days
When it seemed I did not have a friend.
'Cause all I needed was a little faith
So I could catch my breath and face the
World again.

Chorus 2:

Don't forget your second wind.
Wait in your corner until that breeze blows in.

Chorus 3 & 4:

Don't forget your second wind.
Sooner or later you'll feel that momentum kick in.

Uptown Girl

Registration 9
Rhythm: Rock

Words and Music by
Billy Joel

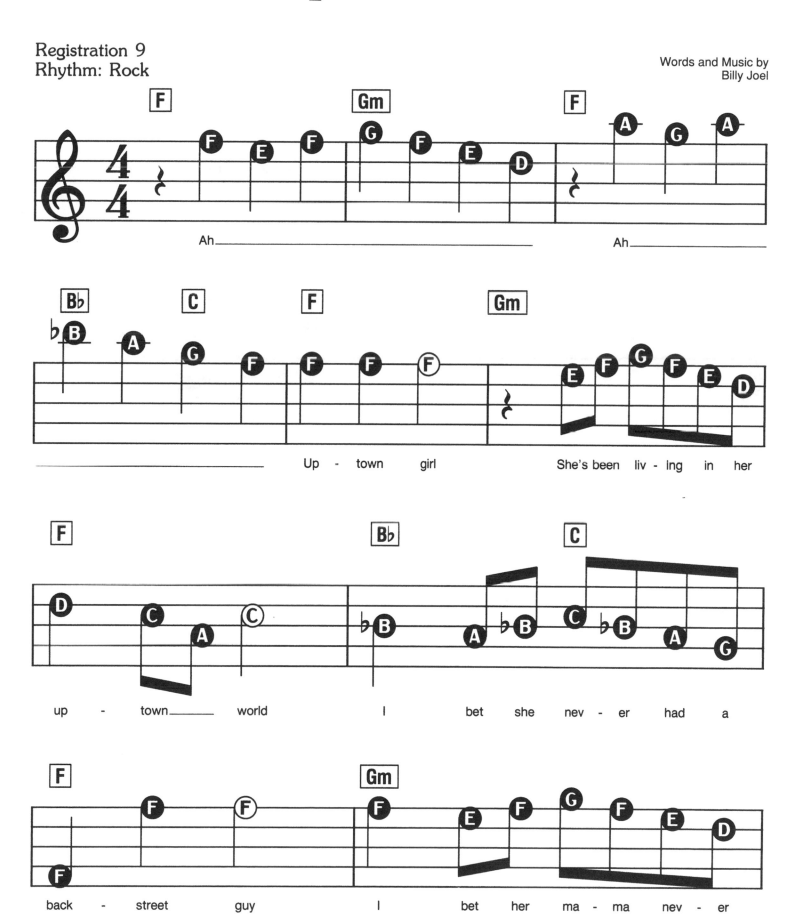

© 1983 JOEL SONGS
All Rights Controlled and Administered by EMI BLACKWOOD MUSIC INC.
All Rights Reserved   International Copyright Secured   Used by Permission

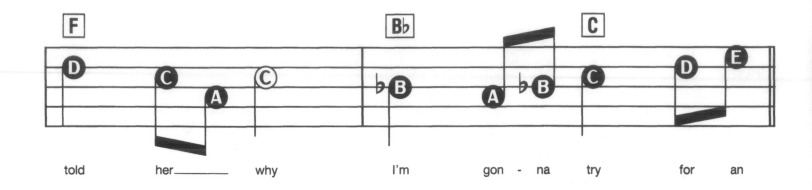

told   her_____ why   I'm   gon - na   try   for   an

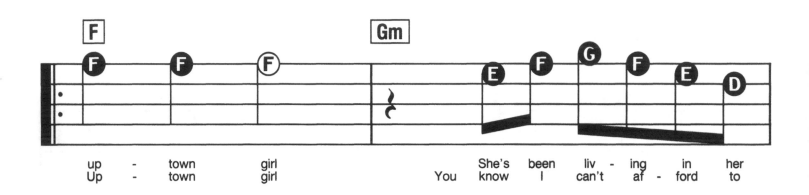

up - town   girl   You   She's   been   liv - ing   in   her
Up - town   girl   know   I   can't   af - ford   to

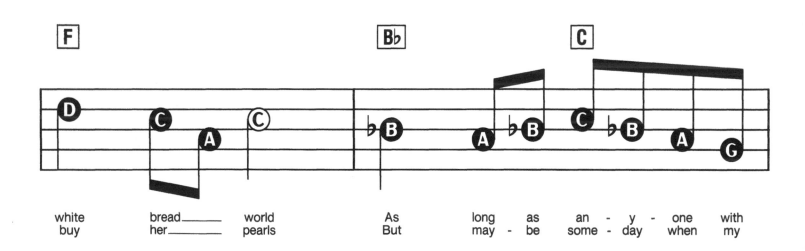

white   bread_____ world   As   long   as   an - y - one   with
buy   her_____ pearls   But   may - be   some - day   when   my

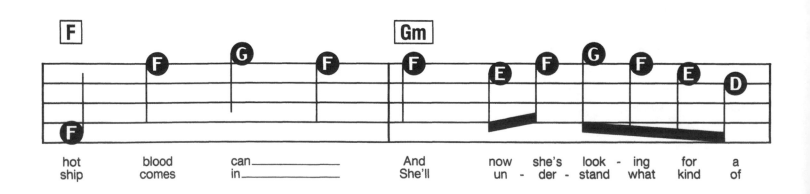

hot   blood   can_____ And   now   she's   look - ing   for   a
ship   comes   in_____ She'll   un - der - stand   what   kind   of

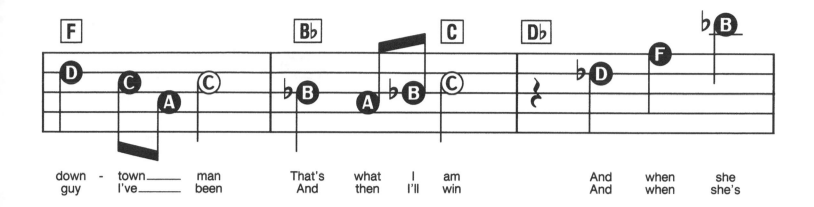

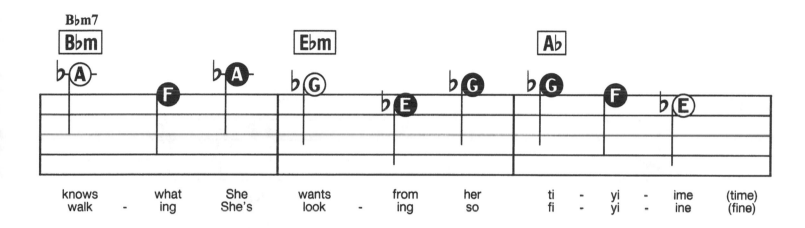

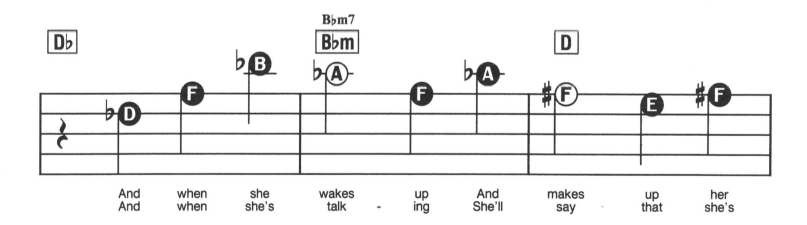

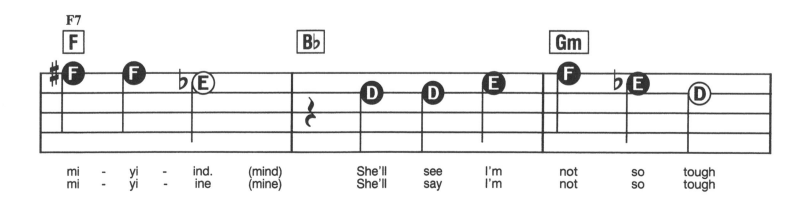

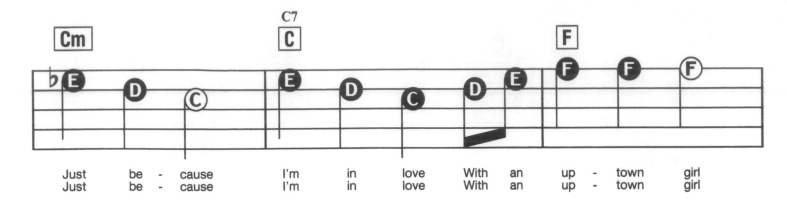

Just be - cause I'm in love With an up - town girl
Just be - cause I'm in love With an up - town girl

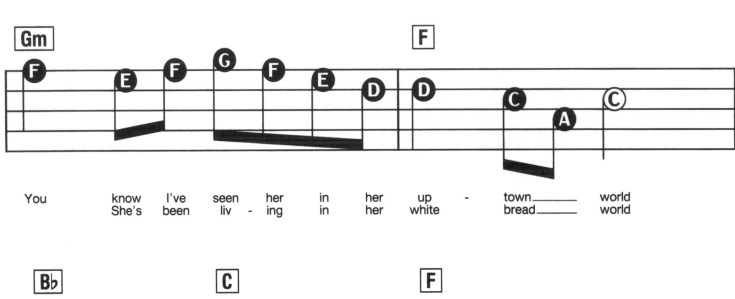

You know I've seen her in her up - town_____ world
She's been liv - ing in her white bread_____ world

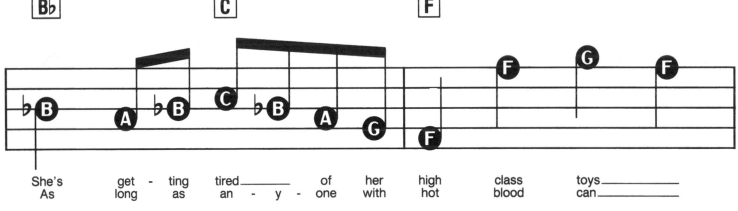

She's get - ting tired_____ of her high class toys_____
As long as an - y - one with hot blood can_____

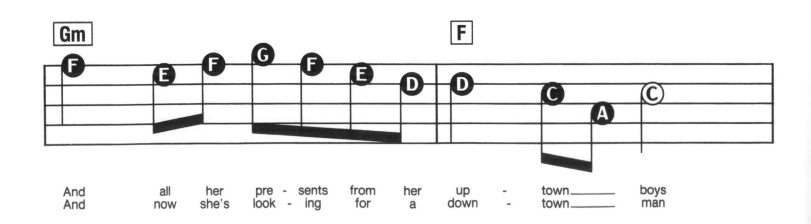

And all her pre - sents from her up - town_____ boys
And now she's look - ing for a down - town_____ man

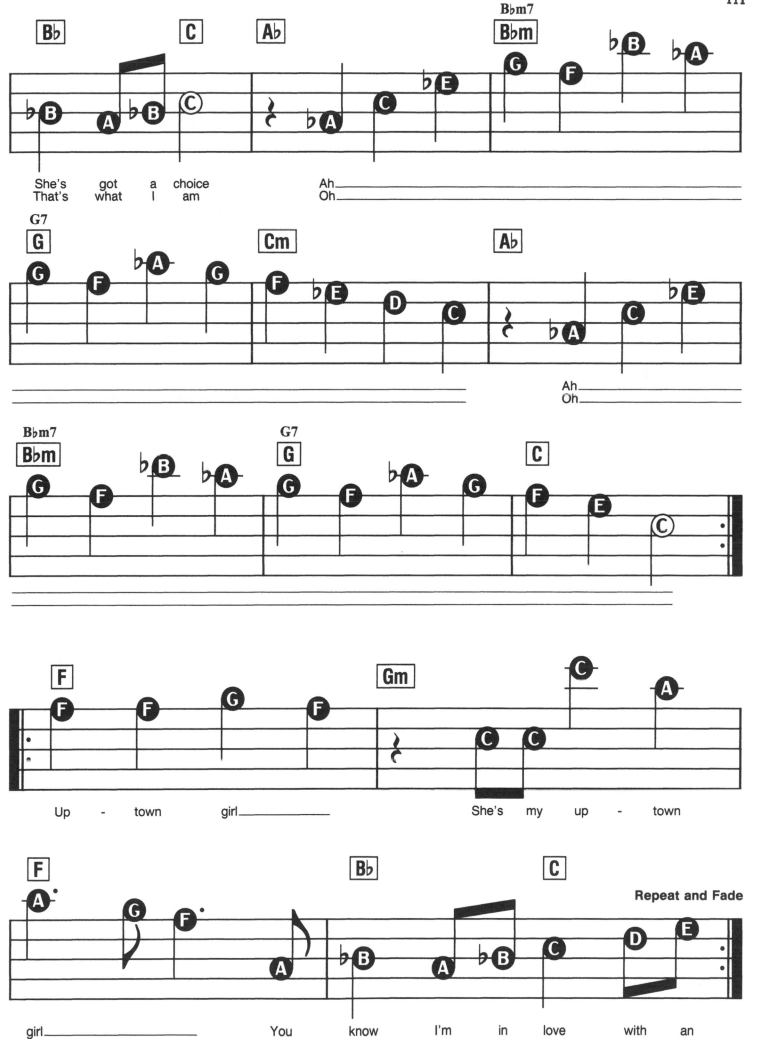

Registration Guide

- Match the Registration number on the song to the corresponding numbered category below. Select and activate an instrumental sound available on your instrument.

- Choose an automatic rhythm appropriate to the mood and style of the song. (Consult your Owner's Guide for proper operation of automatic rhythm features.)

- Adjust the tempo and volume controls to comfortable settings.

Registration

1	Flute, Pan Flute, Jazz Flute
2	Clarinet, Organ
3	Violin, Strings
4	Brass, Trumpet
5	Synth Ensemble, Accordion, Brass
6	Pipe Organ, Harpsichord
7	Jazz Organ, Vibraphone, Vibes, Electric Piano, Jazz Guitar
8	Piano, Electric Piano
9	Trumpet, Trombone, Clarinet, Saxophone, Oboe
10	Violin, Cello, Strings